D1478342

WHAT
IS
GOD
LIKE
?

# WHAT IS GOD LIKE ?

Formerly published as *Strictly Personal*

by

EUGENIA PRICE

ZONDERVAN
PUBLISHING HOUSE

OF THE ZONDERVAN CORPORATION | GRAND RAPIDS, MICHIGAN 49506

Turner Publishing Company
Nashville, Tennessee
www.turnerpublishing.com

What is God Like?

Cover design: Bruce Gore

Library of Congress Cataloging-in-Publication Data Upon Request

9781684426645   paperback
9781684426652   hardback
9781684426669   Ebook


17 18 19 20 10 9 8 7 6 5 4 3 2 1

To
ROSALIND RINKER

# PREFACE

This book will make some readers uneasy. They will fail to find in it, perhaps, some of the familiar jargon of the evangelical world.

It is not written primarily for these persons, who have become so accustomed to a certain method of expressing God that they fail to recognize Him when He is spoken of or written about in the language of the average person. It is the deepest desire of my heart that everyone who reads will make a fresh personal discovery of God as they read. But I have written the book for those who, like myself a few years ago, have not yet considered the tremendous potential of the strictly personal relationship with Him.

In my own contacts with persons who are seeking peace with God, or who are merely seeking a way out of their troubles, I have been keenly aware of the lack of authentic Christian books written in a language which the sincere but untheologically trained person can understand. In *What Is God Like?* I have tried to write such a book.

God made a personal visit to this earth in order to reach people. All kinds of people, with all degrees of

culture and education—or lack of it. He came so that anyone can discover what He is really like! This is not a book
of techniques on how to live the Christian life. I have
personally grown tired of these. It is a book about God
Himself.

I have written it at the end of my first ten years as a
follower of Jesus Christ. In it I have shared from my own
continuing discovery of the nature of the One whom I
follow. I have attempted to communicate in these pages
with those who have become confused or frustrated by
doctrinal explanations; who are, in their hearts, interested
in God, but not in religion as such. I have attempted to
communicate with those who have found themselves unable to cope with their lives, but are in doubt as to what
to do next. I have written the book for persons who wan-
der still in the half-darkness of indecision about what
they really believe; for those who struggle under the
dreadful weight of a distorted concept of the God who
created them.

Fully aware of the risk of arousing the displeasure of
the consciously or unconsciously dogmatic who may read,
I have considered only those who still roam aimlessly outside the awareness of the love of God for each one of
them.

The book will, I hope, also clarify Him for the new
believers who have taken the step of faith but who still
have no basic knowledge of what may lie ahead. I have
not been unmindful, either, of those who are without assurance that their transaction with God is genuine and
eternal.

During the ten years I have been a Christian, I have
come to see some of the ways in which we who follow
Christ are actually blocking those who do not. I have
tried to undo some of the damage we have done in our
ignorance, or our lack of understanding of the state of

mind and heart of a human being out of contact with his Creator.

While I did write *What Is God Like?* primarily for those who are new or still outside the personal relationship with Christ, it is in reality the attempted expression of my own philosophy of life, now that my life is linked with His. I must confess that it has not been difficult for me to express my beliefs as I have expressed them in this book. *This is what I believe.* And it is written in the way in which I best understand it. I have written from no spiritual pedestal. I am not a professional Christian. I am merely another human being, tremendously excited with the fact that God is discoverable to anyone! I hope I have not implied that I have discovered all there is to know about Him. Everyone is always just beginning. Through all eternity, it will be a continuing discovery.

Since it is impossible to write a book from all aspects of the truth at once, may I urge that no one draw a final conclusion—pro or con—until the entire book is read. I ask this of settled believers, new Christians and those who do not yet follow Him. I have tried to allow my philosophy of the Christian life to unfold, rather than to state it bluntly at the outset.

In the main, I have used scriptural quotations from the *Berkeley Version* of the Bible. There is, however, an occasional use of the King James version.

Some of the material in this book appeared in print in my column "Visit with Genie" in the magazine *Faith at Work,* 8 West 40th Street, New York City, and I am grateful for the permission to include it here.

My associate, Rosalind Rinker, to whom I have dedicated this book, has not only managed the mechanics of my manuscript with patience and skill, she has managed to keep discord and interruption at a minimum as I have written, and I am truly grateful.

To Mr. Peter deVisser, my realistic guiding hand at

the Zondervan Publishing House, to the booksellers and other friends who have encouraged me in the writing of this book, I must also say thank you.

To you who read—I shall be constantly hopeful that you will join me in the glorious adventure of discovering what God is really like!

EUGENIA PRICE

*Chicago, Illinois*
*May, 1960*

# CONTENTS

# 1

# The Universal Questioning

# 1

---

# THE UNIVERSAL QUESTIONING

More persons than are willing to admit it live uneasily beneath a row of universal question marks about God.

Those who do not believe use their questions as defenses when, in reality, they can be open doors. Believers shudder in shame when their questions about God are discovered. Somehow the concept seems to be that no one has a right to question God. This is not God's idea!

He encourages questions.

I read recently of a woman with a devout Christian reputation who confessed her secret doubts to her minister. He laughed. "A wonderful Christian like you, Mrs. ——? Why, that's impossible!"

To my mind, he not only slapped her, he also slapped God. Probably this clergyman preaches lustily of a Sunday morning of the lengths to which God has gone to make Himself known to man. And yet, when he was faced with an honest question about God, his own inadequate understanding forced him to duck behind a platitude—even flattery, in order to evade the issue. It would have been impossible for this man to have given a more superficial or unrealistic answer to the woman whose questioning heart had brought her to him for help.

No one is immune to the universal questioning. No one is immune to doubt. No one is all-informed about God and His ways. But anyone can begin to discover Him at any time, *if* that person is open and honest and willing to drop the pretense of being anything but a member of the human race with both the need and the perfect right to discover God firsthand.

The universal questioning is progressive. There are some who still ask—*is* God? Does He exist? Is He a personal God?

Others ask—is God a good God? Can He be a good God and still permit the world to orbit in an atmosphere of sin and suffering and pain?

Some grant the existence of God, but their question extends to a more pertinent point—can I know Him personally? And if so, how? Granted they are convinced of the existence of God, what is the next step? Is it all up to man? Or does man have to wait until some divine whim of God focuses heavenly attention on him?

Is this life on earth all? Or is there more? Do we fight for life in spite of bodies convulsed with pain because this is all there is for us? Or do we fight because the desire for eternal life is created in us?

Is God like the religious people we know? Is He as insensitive as some of His saints? Is He as smug? As remote? As dull? If He is not, what is He like?

How can man worship Someone he doesn't know? How can he place his life in the hands of Someone about whom he harbors so much doubt and uncertainty?

What of the great religions of the world? Which one is the right one? Is one of them the right one? Is religion actually the point after all?

No, it is not.

God is the point. And for all of man's earthly life, he is liable to doubts and questions. But he can *begin* to discover God for himself. Those who have been "set" in their religious beliefs for years can begin to discover Him as He really is at any time. Nothing is required but courage and honesty. No one is safe because of his doctrinal beliefs. But anyone can be safe in the hands of God.

If you are weary of clutching your taught beliefs in your hot and trembling hands, you can drop them any time and begin the adventure of discovering God for yourself.

When you do, you will find that He is holding you. You can stop clutching and rest. The God who created you is in no way dismayed or shocked at your questions. He welcomes them. He created you with an inquiring mind, and He offers Himself openly to you and welcomes your inquiries. This is a *strictly personal* matter between you and God. Even your present interest is His idea.

God is the only living Person who can bear complete inspection. And He lovingly invites it.

# 2

# Can We Know God Personally?

# 2

---

## CAN WE KNOW GOD PERSONALLY?

Anyone can know God personally. Anyone can know His character. Anyone can know His intentions.

I am a Christian because I became convinced at last that God is discoverable.

Dr. J. B. Phillips calls us the "visited planet." We are. If I did not believe that we are, I would by now be involved in no religious pursuit. If I had not become irrevocably convinced that God has personally involved Himself for all time with the human race, I would not be a Christian.

I am a Christian because I now know that God Himself paid a visit to this earth in the Person of Jesus Christ. Around this fact my life is forever centered down.

At the age of thirty-three, I had almost lost interest in finding the key to why I am here. My study of the philosophies had stimulated my mind, but it left my heart empty. My study of many of the other religions of the world left me exhausted. I knew that in me, at least, was not enough desire to "know righteousness" to go through the elaborate intellectual and spiritual gyrations required by them to "reach God."

Metaphysics interested me. But I demanded a great

deal from life in the way of emotional release and fulfillment and the provocative but arid metaphysical prin-
ciples left me longing.

I was bored by Buddhism. I ached for action and the
creative stimulation of personal reaction and desires fulfilled. Nirvana, the sought-for state of desiring nothing,
which is the Buddhist's goal, left me cold and uninter-
ested. I saw quickly that I could never settle for *nothing*.
In my life there would have to be *something*, even if it
destroyed me.

The Analects of Confucius kept my mind occupied
hour after hour. But my heart and my spirit roamed aimlessly, as with the Vedantist's pale, pulseless striving for
contact with some vague All Good.

I plumbed the self-development cults and talked
eagerly with those who felt convinced that everything
lay in the realm of our minds, positive and negative. I
saw some hope here, since in many ways life seemed to
back it up. But when I saw the ardent followers of the
All Good Universal Mind capable of the same variety
of venom as mine when their rights were stepped on, I
began to pull away. More than that, I deeply feared
death, either my own or the death of the few people
whom I really loved. And nothing about an intellectual
refusal to accept death as reality even remotely began
to dissolve the fear that fastened more tightly around my
heart with each passing year.

Up to then nothing really tragic had happened to me.
But I was realistic enough to know that no human being
is immune to tragedy and suffering and death. In philosophy and in religion I hunted almost feverishly for
some answer to the heartbreak I knew was up ahead for
me. (As you read the pages of this book, you will learn
how my fear was gradually loosened on this point.)

Perhaps most of all, I was concerned (when I dared
to face it) with the wild horses of my own make-up.

Everything I tried, no matter how carefully or how skillfully, left me eventually, still searching. Would I always be restless and uneasy when I was alone and quiet? Would I always have to wonder why I had chosen to earn my living by writing words for other people to read and hear, when around my own heart I dragged the sometimes intolerable weight of my own enormous question mark about life?

Metaphysics and self-development and the philosophy of the Vedantists did not hold me. I had no desire to escape life. I wanted more of it! I was willing to take my chances on the suffering and the heartbreak if only I could find enough of it to fill the gaping space, empty of everything but my giant question mark.

In retrospect, I see now that I was more than willing to open my arms and my heart and my mind to anything that seemed vital enough. The trouble was—nothing did for long. I longed to worship something or someone. I loved literature and writing and for many years I worshiped the muse herself. But she was utterly dependent upon me! And I knew I was not dependable enough to satisfy my constant longing.

My life was often interesting, often highly enjoyable, often fulfilling. But not for long. Ultimately, I would find myself alone again and forced to think. And to know that although I had searched diligently, I had not found.

Time after time I gave myself wholly to one idea or another. To one pursuit or another. Time after time I found that the thing to which I had so wholeheartedly given myself, had dwindled away.

Soon there was little or nothing there.

And then, by a set of circumstances related in my book, *The Burden Is Light,* I discovered to my great, glad amazement that I could know God!

I hadn't thought of Him much in ten years, but swiftly and relentlessly my heart began to be dented by one divine impact after another. Gentle at first, the realization blows increased in strength and I was at last graciously struck to my knees. Not in shame at once, but literally struck to my knees by the sudden shock of realizing that although I hadn't thought about God at all for ten years, He had never once taken His thoughts from me.

He loved me. He had lovingly and carefully and slowly brought me to the only place of potential fulfillment for anyone—face to face with Himself.

So sharply did the realization of His love strike me that my old question of the existence of a Personal God dropped away without my noticing.

There He was confronting me.

Of His existence I then had no doubt. Of His holiness, I had no doubt. Of His power, I had no doubt. But what was His heart really like? Would He remain remote and holy and high? Would He keep me on my knees fighting off the shame and the guilt which slowly began to cover me?

Was this what God had to offer?

I felt helpless, weak, unworthy. It was depressing, frightening, confusing.

I was undone. I had come apart at all my well-guarded seams. I knew I would never amount to anything without Him, and yet this was my life He was demanding! The most precious thing I had ever owned. At that moment it seemed more precious than ever before.

Had He really known all about me through the years in which I searched? Could He really know what would fulfill my longing? Surely I had never, never been so attracted to anything or anyone before. But could I really trust Him? What of all the suffering in the world? The tragedy? Did He care about it? Did He really understand human nature? Could God possibly know what it's like to be one of us down here?

Even if I agreed to the fact that He was a Creator God, how could I be sure that anyone great enough to create a complex human being could know how it feels to *be* one? To be trapped in a body on an earth full of strong down-pulls and—all right, I would even use the words I had long ago struck from my vocabulary: How could He know what it's like to be tempted to sin? To worry? To be afraid?

For a long time I had to put aside anyone's concept of the Cross and the theology of redemption. I was much more concerned with God Himself. Was it possible to *know* this One who demanded to be my Master?

Could any human being ever really know God personally?

Could I learn something of how His mind worked? Or was I supposed to stay on my knees with my head down and just trust without actually knowing much about the Person who asked me to give Him my life?

This is the place He longs to bring each one of us at least once in our lives. Because even above His Cross, even above His work of redemption, even above a desire for eternal life, He wants us to be concerned with Him personally.

It is not God's way to tell a struggling human being that he is to believe simply because God is God. He asks no one to accept grief and tragedy and suffering patiently just because He is who He is. He wants us to know what He's like! For this very reason God paid a visit to the earth. He knows that no human heart can trust Him in the deep places until that human heart knows Him *as He is.*

He doesn't expect it of anyone.

God prefers honest rebellion to the whipped dog acquiescence of a human being just because it is supposed to be the pious thing to do.

He limited Himself to our earthly existence in the

Person of Jesus of Nazareth, so no one from any background would ever again have to wonder about Him.

All that could be contained of God in a human being broke into human history when Jesus was born. Think through the Old Testament. Or, if you haven't read it yet, consider this: Over and over again, God's chosen people misunderstood Him. They felt duty bound to obey Him, and for short periods they did fairly well at it. Then off they would go again on another idolatrous riot of disobedience and rebellion. God understood this. And so He came Himself, in Jesus Christ, to set us straight about Himself once and for all.

Did God reveal Himself fully in Jesus Christ?

Yes, He did. John wrote in the first chapter of his Gospel, "No one has ever seen God; (but) the only-begotten Son, who abides at the Father's bosom, He has made Him known."

God has seen to it that to every man and woman and child, He is *knowable*. He knew He had to make Himself available and knowable in a way we could grasp. We can know another human being. This is not beyond us spiritually. And since He knows our capacities and our limitations as no other living person, He visited the earth because He had to visit it. There was no other way in which we could grasp fully the true intentions of our Heavenly Father toward us all.

Anyone, anywhere, can know God personally through Jesus Christ. Anyone, anywhere, can know God's intentions toward the whole human race. Now that I know this, although my questions are not all answered, my giant question mark has somehow disappeared. After ten years of belonging to Jesus Christ, I know now that at last I have unreservedly given myself to Someone who will not dwindle away.

"Lo, I am with you always."

# 3

# What Is the Good News?

# 3

---

## WHAT IS THE GOOD NEWS?

Here is a question which everyone should consider well. Christians should consider it for their own sakes and for the sake of those still outside the personal awareness of God's love in Christ. Those still unaware of God in Christ have every right to ask if there really is any "good news" to be told. And when they ask, their answer should be more definite than merely to say the "good news" is the Gospel, or a plan of salvation, or a means of eternal life.

Exactly what is the "good news"? What is the Gospel?

How were the hopes and fears of all the years met in the ancient town of Bethlehem where Jesus was born? What does that really mean? What does Christianity actually have to offer a man? We need to pinpoint the "good news" carefully.

Surely there is nothing worthwhile in a life without hope.

There is nothing worthwhile in a life riddled with fear.

Indeed it would be good news to anyone if it were a fact that in one event—in the birth of one person—hope could spring to life and fears could be met and done away with. But is this true? Were the hopes and fears of every person met in the birth of Jesus Christ that first Christmas? Have we allowed this to be the central fact

17

of the good news? Or have we tucked it into the side pocket of mere theological concept? In attempting to explain the Gospel, have we limited it to mere religion and divorced most of man's everyday life from God? Why is it that we get bogged down in pious attempts to sell certain promised "effects" of religious belief, when we have access to the very Cause of the "good news"?

In other words, why do we go on selling salvation and the victorious life, when the Saviour Himself said, "I, if I be lifted up . . . will draw all men unto me"?

The "good news" has always been, and will always be, that God is discoverable. He is not asking us to follow Him with no notion of what He is really like. He went to the greatest lengths to show Himself as He is. He seemed determined to leave no loopholes. God Himself has already done everything in His power to make Himself known to us.

This is the "good news."

The only possible way to find out how our hopes and fears are met in Him is to discover His true character. The more I see down into the heart of God, the more rapidly my fears melt away. The more I see of His intentions toward the entire human race, the higher hope springs within me. The more I learn of Him, the more able I am to accept the inner rest which Jesus promised.

We stop too soon in His great invitation to everyone, "Come to me all you who labor and are heavily burdened and I will rest you." Jesus said much more: "Take my yoke upon you and *learn of me.*" As plainly as possible He explained that He understood that no one can rest in a relationship with another person about whom he knows little or nothing. God Himself, through Jesus Christ, was urging us to find out what He is really like. He knew He could bear inspection.

He longs to reveal Himself to anyone. And revelation from God is not a static, abstract thing. Men and women discover God from entering into a personal relationship with Him. We learn of God as we learn of each other. By being together. When Jesus urged us to learn of Him, He did not mean that we were to sit down and wait for spiritual lightning to strike. Christians do not have to labor for the Zen Buddhist's *satori* or stage of enlightenment. We are to come to Him expectantly and allow Him, with the cooperation of our open hearts, to show us through a living relationship with Himself what He is like.

We have already said that a trip through the Old Testament demonstrates the necessity for God's invasion of human history. He came because He knew we would not be able to find out enough about His true nature any other way. He came to erase forever the ugly marks on the hearts of His loved ones who struggle with distorted ideas of a God of vengeance. He came to strike vengeance from the vocabulary of humanity, on His part and on ours. When we finally see Christ as God in the flesh, we are enabled to let go even the desire for vengeance. Once we see that God is love, once we catch on to what Jesus strained every nerve to show us about the true nature of the Heavenly Father, we no longer fear vengeance. And we are no longer driven to avenge ourselves.

Once we look deeply into the heart of God as we see it in Jesus Christ, we are enabled to forsake the luxury of hatred and self-pity.

Once we know something of God's real intentions toward all mankind in Jesus Christ, we begin to see that all that matters ultimately is that a God like this is in charge!

The success or failure of all of life is directly dependent upon our knowledge of what God is really like. Therefore, the heart of the "good news" is that God's heart has been laid open for us to see His true nature. The "good news" is that God is what Jesus declared Him to be. The "good news" is the very nature of God Himself.

# 4

# Does God Know Us Personally?

# 4

---

# DOES GOD KNOW US PERSONALLY?

No matter what you know or believe about Jesus Christ, everything He knows and believes about you is true.

You may or may not believe that He was God Himself breaking into human history almost two thousand years ago, but this in no way diminishes His intense minute by minute concern for you.

You may or may not be aware of Him. But He is, at this very moment, sharply aware of you.

He knows you—as you are.

He knows what you could have made of your life. He knows what you have made of it. He knows the reason behind every failure, behind every success. He knows the consequences of your failures. He knows the effects of every success. It is no mystery to Him how your failures and successes have marked you.

If you have lacked human love and companionship, He knows about it. If you have been coddled by someone who "meant you well" but who weakened you to the point where you find it difficult to make a decision on your own, He knows about that. If you are a strong human personality and proud of it, He knows this, too.

If life has offered you more tragedy than joy, this is

no secret to God. If you are suffering physically, so that every new day stretches away pain-dimmed and heavy, He knows. He knows about your fear, all the way from its cause to its devastating effect upon you now. He is the God of the shaking hand and the tormented mind. He is the God of the heart torn by grief and the eyelids swollen from weeping. "Jesus wept." And He still remembers the tight pressure of the heavy heart; the distorted way the world looks through eyes filled with tears.

We do not need to explain ourselves to Him. He already knows.

We are often a mystery to one another. Deceiving our fellow human beings is an easy thing to do. Deceiving ourselves is even easier. There isn't a person who is not in some way self-deceived. In each one is at least a tinge of the neurotic. Some have refused for so long to accept life realistically that all power to see it as it is seems lost. These, the psychologist calls genuine neurotics. God is a realist. He is the only Person who can bear to look realistically at things as they are and people as they are. But He can bear it and He does.

He knows all that is good and all that is bad in you. He knows all that is good and all that is bad in me. God is not deceivable. "He knows what is in man." And He begins from there.

If you are a new Christian and some well meaning person is right now attempting to pour you quickly into a mold before you "cool off," thank him for his effort, but do not be confused by it. No human being can know you as you really are. And the Christian life is a life lived in a *strictly personal* relationship with God Himself through Jesus Christ.

If you have just met Christ, relax. There is no possible way for you to know Him fully yet. But He brought His own love into your heart when He came, and with this love of His you can learn to understand and forgive those who seem to be pushing you toward a stifling, unrealistic conformity.

Each human being is conditioned by his own particular background and environment. Even those who have known Jesus Christ personally for many years are still, in one sense, apt to be victims of some man-devised marginal emphasis. Remember this, if you are new in the Christian life. Everything you are told to do or think by some Christian friend or counselor is not necessarily God's preferred way to deal with you. Allow your mind to grasp this early and start now to form the habit of going straight to Him for counsel. Learn of Christ Himself in the Scriptures. Talk to Him in prayer. Jesus Himself said He would send the Holy Spirit, the Counselor, to teach you.

We need one another, but new and old Christians alike need to realize that only God knows each heart's actual condition. Only God knows the depth of the old patterns formed in and out of the Christian life. Conformity is not the key to the dynamic Christian life. Jesus Christ Himself is Christianity. He is alive. He got up and walked out of that tomb. He is eternally involved with every human life, and He is involved with your life as it is now. Not as you want to make it, not as someone keeps telling you to make it. Christ is involved with you as you are. He is realistic with you and He will remain realistic.

Other human beings can change us superficially, where our outward behavior is concerned. Only Christ can change us at the center of our beings. And I have found that He does this according to our cooperation and according to His own timetable. Not that He hesitates for one and hurries with another for some cosmic reason of His own. I have found Him to be utterly realistic in His procedure. His timetable is set according to what He really knows about us.

Whatever the length of time involved in your personal

walk with God, He is still working in the depths of your personality according to what He knows is there. Realization of this, if you are a new Christian, will prevent you from making the always fatal blunder of putting on a pedestal someone who has known Him a long time. Realization of this, if you are a long-time follower, will stop you short if you have unwittingly been "playing God" and trying to convert someone yourself.

Every person who has become involved consciously in the life with Christ needs to remember that we are all in school with Him. No one has graduated. We are all on the way. No one has arrived. He is every minute intensely and equally concerned in the deep places with us all.

A new Christian said to me not long ago, "Why, I never think of praying for you to grow in your spiritual life—I figure you've got it made!"

What a ghastly distortion of the truth about the Christian life. Christians are merely people who have finally waked up to the frightening fact of their own desperate needs! And we remain only this. We remain just people still in need of a Saviour. Those who are believers have Him, but this does not lessen their need for Him.

When I stand on a platform and talk about Him, He speaks through me to the people, in spite of my own weaknesses and personality twists. He is working with me, too. Just as He is working with you, with us all—as we drive our automobiles, ride trains, read our Bibles and newspapers, cook dinner, pound typewriters, speak from platforms, pray, make business decisions and sleep. "He who hath begun a good work in you, will bring it to completion. . . ."

And He knows us all—as we are.

I think I love and admire Jesus' disciple, John, most of all the disciples. But I am more like Peter, as you may know yourself to be. And I have learned much about God

Himself through tracing His actions and attitudes toward Peter.

Just as He knows all that is well intentioned and all that is satanic in us, He also knew it about Peter. The word *satan* in Hebrew merely means *adversary*. Anything that is in itself adverse to God or to man is in the simplest sense *satanic*. Since God is for us, anything that harms or degrades us is against us, an adversary, therefore *satanic*. Jesus, when He was on earth, did not look at outward signs of righteousness or unrighteousness. Today, He still works with the inward adversaries of God and man, which only He can see and which only He fully understands.

Peter was impetuous, perhaps hot-headed and emotionally unstable, but generally sincere. He was ready to try anything. But, like most of us, he only succeeded some of the time. Peter's story is a striking description of God Himself. Jesus gave him the name Peter, which means little rock. And as we live along with Peter through some of his ups and down, we begin to see clearly—not Peter, but His Lord, who Himself is the unshakable Rock.

Peter hit extreme spiritual highs and lows, but I am convinced that none of it surprised the Master. He knew Peter. Not as Peter thought he was. Not as the other disciples considered him, but as he was. Peter vacillated just as we do. One day up, the next day down. But nothing he did or did not do in any way altered God's attitude toward him.

One day when Jesus and His disciples "entered the region of Caesarea Philippi, He asked his disciples, Who do people say the Son of Man is?"

This is the question of questions. To its answer is hinged God's complete estimate of man. To its answer is hinged man's estimate of God. So far as we know, this is the first time the question was ever voiced by Jesus.

And that day, in the outskirts of the little city near Mount Hermon, it was answered. At first, there was a babble of typical snap-judgments and downright hearsay. The disciples, we are told in Matthew's account, apparently all began talking at once: "Some say, John the Baptist; others, Elijah; others, Jeremiah, or one of the prophets."

Jesus pinned them down. "He asked them, but who do you say that I am?"

There must have been a long, sharp silence. Then Simon Peter answered, "Thou art the Christ, the Son of the living God."

Peter had gone straight to the heart of everything. His answer was not only right, it contained God's total answer to every human problem. It shouted across the years to every listening heart that God is discoverable at last!

I'm sure Peter was a little proud. He might even have swaggered a bit, trying to look pious at the same time. After all, he was the one who said it. Had he leaped ahead of the others spiritually? Perhaps, in his own considered opinion. After all, Jesus answered him, "Blessed are you, Simon Bar-Jonah." But because He knew Peter, and to save him from the satanic "adversary" of pride, He reminded him that it was not flesh and blood that revealed this to Peter, but His Heavenly Father.

This was Peter's highest point. It was the high point in history, in fact. A human being had recognized his Creator in the flesh! And right there Jesus gave Simon the name of Peter, and said that on the unmovable rock of Peter's statement of truth, He would build His Church.

Peter, like many of us on our good days, was in tune with heaven, and heaven revealed itself.

But if we read on in the same chapter of Matthew's account, we find Jesus telling His disciples that He must "leave for Jerusalem and suffer much from the elders, priests and scribes, and be killed and raised again on the third day." This was too much for Peter. Even with his new "spiritual progress," he grabbed matters in his own hands and, "leading Him aside, undertook to remonstrate with Him: Mercy on you, Lord; this must never happen to You!"

I can see Peter pull the Lord almost roughly to one side to scold Him. "This is ridiculous, Master. Nothing like this should happen to You. Why, look who You are!"

Jesus Christ, God in human form, turned and faced Peter. With the same concern for him as a few moments before, He said, "Peter, you get behind me, Satan, you are a snare to Me; for you are not minding things divine, but things human."

This same complex Peter, who had heard from heaven as he identified the Son of the living God, had suddenly become earthbound! He was no longer tuned to heaven. He was "minding things human."

Does this sound familiar? Do we not often grasp spiritual truth in our quiet times with God and within an hour or less lose our tempers or take things into our own hands like "adversaries of God"? Like "satans"?

Does this surprise God?

Not at all. He knows us, *as we are*. Just as He knew Peter.

Did it change Jesus' love for Peter? Not at all. At the moment the hard-muscled, headstrong fisherman declared Jesus to be God's Son, Jesus knew the later moment of spiritual confusion would come.

The day He chose Peter, along with James and John, to see His Transfiguration on the mountain, He knew that on the darkest night, when He most needed a human hand to clasp His, Peter would fall asleep in shadow-streaked Gethsemane. After the Last Supper, when Peter vowed vehemently that even if every other man on earth would forsake Him, he, Peter would not, Jesus knew what was in Peter's heart. Here He saw an incongruous mixture, such as He often sees in our hearts. Peter meant it when he said he would never forsake Jesus. As far as Peter knew himself at that moment, he was sincere. But Jesus quietly told Peter that before the rooster crowed the next morning he would deny his Master three times. On the dusty road outside of Caesarea Philippi, when Peter exclaimed, "Thou art the Christ, the Son of the living God," Jesus knew that the third time Peter denied Him during His dark night, he would swear about it to make his denial stick.

Did Peter's blasphemy change Jesus' love for him?

No.

On the morning He rose from the dead and left the sealed tomb forever, He left word with the angel who said, "Go, tell His disciples *and Peter* that He precedes you into Galilee."

He wanted to make sure that Peter knew his Master's love had not changed. He longs to make sure that we know that He knows us *as we are,* and that His love for us does not change. That it is in no way diminished or increased according to our defeats or victories, our so-called backsliding or progress.

He knows us—as we are. Faithless and faithful. Trusting and doubting. Accepting and resisting. Blessing and cursing. And only Jesus Christ knows how to change us where we need changing. Only He knows where to begin and how to continue.

He knows that we do not "make progress" with Him. It is He who makes progress with us! And we never surprise Him either way.

He knows us and can bear to look at us and live with us—as we are.

# 5

# Is God Shockable?

# 5

## IS GOD SHOCKABLE?

I am convinced that when for any reason a Christian becomes discouraged in his spiritual life he is forgetting or falling a victim to his own ignorance of what God is really like.

It has been said that discouragement is the devil's best weapon with the follower of Christ. I agree. But one clear realization about God can make this so-called weapon forever useless: God is not shockable!

Christians waste time languishing in pools of depression over their spiritual states because they occasionally know periods of doubt. I am inclined to believe that anyone who never doubts is not really thinking. God is not confused by our honest doubts. Why should we be confused? There is no way to learn truth unless one first approaches the subject with some doubt or uncertainty. Scientific discovery would stop abruptly if every scientist suddenly decided that he had once and for all settled all questions involved in the physical universe.

Jesus Christ is every moment ready and willing to reveal Himself to those who seek honestly to know Him, but He is in no way surprised or shocked at the doubts which sometimes interrupt our daily discovery of Him.

The more I read of Him in the Gospel accounts, the more I am convinced that He prefers to be confronted by an honest doubter who wants to see Him as He is. Over and over He made it clear that He is concerned with clarifying central issues for each individual on a personal basis. He went the whole way with "doubting Thomas," but He said some of His most disparaging things about the "hypocrites" who followed the pattern of established religious worship merely because it was established.

He is not shocked at our doubts, but I do believe He is grieved when we become bogged down by them. He is not discouraged with us when we are discouraged with ourselves.

Once and for all, we should have it straight that God is never surprised, discouraged or shocked by us.

He is realistic with us at all times.

This in no way gives us license to side-step His demands upon our lives. But it does wipe any further need for discouragement out of the picture. Once I saw clearly that no matter how I felt or what I did, it in no way changed Jesus Christ, I was set free from ever again being discouraged with my own sweet spiritual self! I was off my own hands as never before. I was suddenly on Jesus Christ as never before.

"While we were yet sinners, Christ died for us." He didn't wait for us to improve ourselves. He died for us as we are. And since His death was motivated by His love, and since "God is love," how could our doubts and depressions possibly affect the flow of this love toward us? God does not go away from us during our disobedient periods. It is we who get lost in the maze of our own introspection.

It is extremely important for both new and older Christians to know that God is *not* shockable.

We shock one another, but God is unshockable simply because He knows us as we were yesterday, as we are today and as we will be tomorrow. He is fully aware that we are still mere human beings. And even though He longs to see us come to the place of realizing our tremendous potential with our lives linked to His, still He waits always nearby, until we do see. The Christian life is not a subjective struggle to reach a place of high grace. It is the simple seeing that grace in Jesus Christ has already reached to us in our present condition.

Out pour our prayers of much talking as we ridiculously remind God of what He already knows about us. "O God, I am such a weak person. My need is so great." True. And this is a right prayer. But when we begin to dwell on our weakness and to stay in the rut of discouragement as though He didn't know about it at all, we are wrong.

If you do something which shocks you and sends you into a fit of depression about yourself, you are saying in effect that you are surprised to discover that you are not the tremendous Christian you thought you were. This is pride. The smooth Christian life is one which sees its need, accepts it and goes on depending solely on the fact that He is always at work through His Holy Spirit, untangling and redeeming the source of the trouble.

The forgiveness of Jesus Christ is an active thing. It is in no way passive. Some of us are inclined to consider forgiveness lightly. We are passive in our asking for it and we are passive—almost casual—in our acceptance. This is not dealing in forgiveness from the standpoint of the Cross, either from His side or from ours. When we see our dreadful need, we are rightly dismayed and sick at heart. But this is different from being shocked and discouraged.

When we begin to see ourselves as we are, in contrast with Jesus Christ as He is, our need can seem to smother us at first. We are not to stop here in our insight, because if we do we skid inevitably into the rut of discouragement with ourselves.

It is here that we must look at Him as He is, and realize that if we did not have this disease of sin within us He would not have needed to go to the Cross. We do have it, He did go to the cross and forgiveness remains costly to God; but it *remains*. Not as a "thing" to be dealt with passively or casually. It is a part of the Person who gave Himself.

When we ask a human being whom we love for forgiveness, we experience shame, remorse, sorrow. But when we know forgiveness has been given by that person, our hearts leap up with hope and gratitude. Hope because we know that loved one has confidence that we will not do it again; and gratitude because the loved one loved enough to give up any right to hold our sin against us. This is not a casual process. It is an active, pain and love filled exchange.

God is not surprised and He is not shocked by us in any way. He is concerned and ready to heal, give and forgive with the recklessness of love found only in the heart of God. And then He wants and has every right to expect us to go on. No one can go far with a heavy burden of discouragement and "disenchanted self-love" chained to his back. Jesus said, "Come unto me, all ye that . . . are heavy laden and I will give you rest."

Who can rest when he is not relaxed?

If you are biting your spiritual lip and clenching your spiritual fist in despair and disillusionment over the way you have turned out, you cannot rest. If you are straining every nerve to live up to someone's idea of evangelical conformity, you cannot rest. If you are "trying to be a good Christian," you have missed the point of Jesus' lovely offer. The Christian life in its truest sense is a life lived in expectancy from God. We are confronted in the New Testament with the absolute demands of God's

Kingdom. But the mood of the New Testament is not the mood of so many evangelical Christians. It is not a mood of condemnation. The New Testament makes plain the rightful demands of the Saviour God, but it does it in a mood of hope and expectancy *from* that God. Every claim of Christ upon the life of any person is rooted in His love. He has not laid down abstract laws to cause us strain. He has given Himself to us, so that we can rest.

John Knox wrote, "The God who asks everything is eager also to give everything. His moral demands are absolute, but He forgives to the uttermost." He took on your total personality when He took you to Himself. He didn't just take your good intentions or your bad ones. He took you. All of you. As you are. And with your total personality, He is constantly working His great redemptive work whether you see results or not.

It is a comfort to receive greeting cards and hang up plaques which remind us that God understands. He does. But how much better for us o *accept* the fact of His understanding once and for all and proceed from there!

Comfort is a needed thing for us all. But it is only a part of the wonder which can be ours when we realize at last and put to practical use, the fact of His total understanding. To say that someone understands does not necessarily mean that he approves. But it does do away with the highest barrier to any relationship—the possibility of recoil when one person involved is shocked.

Much of my mail comes from young people who are afraid to confide in their parents or ministers or teachers. "I know I should tell my mother about this, but she would be shocked."

An alcoholic man wrote not long ago, "I went to my minister for help, but he was shocked that I'd be so low and ungrateful as to keep on drinking after such a wonderful girl as my wife agreed to marry me."

I love to answer letters like those, because I can assure these people that Jesus Christ never recoils from anything. If this had been in His nature, He would surely have recoiled from the shame and horror of His Cross.

To you who are new Christians, my heart reaches through the pages of this book to assure you that although you may shock your spiritual human friend (because after all he or she is only human) you do not, you cannot, shock God. He is always there with His heart and His mind perfectly open to you. Not necessarily with approval or sanction of what you have done or thought, but open to you as you are in your need. We are shocked by things which we cannot imagine ourselves doing. Jesus Christ was tempted in all points as we are tempted, when He was on earth. He was sinless, but temptation does not shock Him. Not only because He was tempted Himself, but because the great Creator did become our Saviour and He knows human nature as no one else can know it. It is not hard for Him to imagine our doing anything.

He is a realist.

Since He created the human mind, the unreality of neuroticism is no mystery to Him. He longs for us to be honest with Him and with ourselves. With His strength to use, we can face ourselves more realistically. And reality is the key to allowing Him to make progress with us. He will be realistic with us at all times. He can be no other way and remain true to His nature, which is an all knowing one.

*O Lord, thou hast searched me, and known me.*
*Thou knowest my downsitting and mine uprising,*
*Thou understandest my thought afar off.*
*Thou compassest my path and my lying down,*
*and art acquainted with all my ways.*
　　　　　　　　　　　　　*—Psalm 139: 1, 2, 3 (KJV)*

If He seems not to be answering your prayers in a certain area, nine times out of ten it is because you are not yet being realistic about something.

Jesus Christ is never satisfied with a superficial invasion of our lives. He does not approve of an adulterous relationship, but just breaking it off is not enough for Him, because He knows the inner damage can go on with you unless you see realistically why it should be broken off. He will not force you to break it off, but He will enlighten you so that you will come to see it His way, *if* you will be honest with Him. He knows that to hold lustful, covetous thoughts about a wrong relationship can be just as damaging as the relationship itself. And in all of His dealings with you, He is primarily concerned about you, not about your keeping certain laws for the sake of the law itself.

Other Christians may be shocked that you are involved in a particular situation. But happily, some are more realistic about the nature of sin and of God. A young woman once told me about a talk she had with an elderly lady who had lived a moral Christian life. The young woman confided to her that she was struggling to break off an illicit affair. "I'm sorry to have to burden you with this story, and I suppose you're shocked, but I do need help."

"Shocked?" the old lady chuckled. "No, dear. Sin is sin. Your affair is no more shocking than my critical tongue can be!"

This old saint had seen reality in the light that shines from the Cross of Calvary for anyone who will look.

A sincere, hard working W.C.T.U. woman approached my mother not long ago with a severe reprimand because she had not been active in the work lately. Mother had a legitimate reason, but in order to reassure the lady, she tried bringing up my interest in our farm for alcoholics. She also told of having tried to help an alcoholic friend, hoping for the old lady's interest. Instead of interest

Mother got a snort of disapproval! "I wouldn't have one
of those drunken people in my house for a minute!"

This does not mirror the general attitude of the good
ladies in the W.C.T.U. by any means. But it did show
that even though our doctrine may be "correct" and our
energies spent in "good causes," if we are still shockable
by anything human nature does, we are missing the point
of Calvary.

No one ever needs to fear God's recoil from anything.
Or anyone.

The thief on the cross who turned to Jesus found this
to be true. The Lord knew this man's heart and knew
why his criminal record was what it was. He was not
shocked that the man dared to ask from a criminal's cross
to be remembered when Christ came into His Kingdom.
Jesus was nailed to the same kind of cross. He could not
reach His hand to the fellow, it was nailed down. But He
was still Love. And His love reached out and assured the
thief that with no further delay or ceremony, he would
be with Him that very day in Paradise.

He moved toward the penitent thief that dark afternoon with all the love of His breaking heart. But to those
who know Him as He is, this is just what one would expect Him to do. After all, God is love. And love is always
in motion toward the loved one. To be shocked is to
recoil.

Love never recoils. It reaches out to heal.

# 6

## What Is He Really Like?

# 6

---

# WHAT IS HE REALLY LIKE?

Wherever my questions begin, they ultimately either disappear, or are answered directly as I "grow in the knowledge of the Lord Jesus Christ."

He Himself was God in the flesh. "In the beginning was the Word, and the Word was with God, and the Word was God. . . . And the Word was made flesh and dwelt among us."

Most people come to believe that Jesus Christ was God's revelation of Himself—was God in the flesh, because the Bible says so. This was a large factor in my own first frightened leap of faith over this otherwise uncrossable chasm where Jesus stretches Himself between us and the Father. Now after ten years, I know the Bible declares Him to be the Son of God, simply because it is true. Once we make the leap "over" with our eternal weight on Christ, we not only find ourselves at peace with God, we find all of life backing up our faith.

Jesus Christ was God Himself come to earth, or He was not. This is the one point where the leap of faith is required. Either we believe Him or we don't. There is no middle ground. But once, by faith, we make this leap, we find Him there and all else begins to fall into place. If

43

you believe that God invaded human history in the Person of Jesus of Nazareth, you are a Christian. After that initial leap of faith in His identity, all other necessary faith comes to you as a result of your *continuing discovery* of what Jesus Christ is like.

If you know a person to be trustworthy after steady association with this person, faith in him is no problem. It is automatic. The more you discover about Jesus Christ, the more you will find your faith increasing.

Halfhearted, timid, defeated Christians are those who have not set themselves to discover God Himself. True Christian enthusiasm cannot be whipped up by loud preaching or loud singing. Noisy Christians are not necessarily dynamic Christians. They may even be basically timid or halfhearted. The Christians who attract us and remind us most of their Master are the quiet, sure, bold ones. And quiet, confident, holy-boldness is not achieved by noisy self-effort, or by thinking holy or bold thoughts. The peace and naturalness and calm of those contagious saints come as a simple result of their willingness to find out more and more of what God is like.

A clamorous "defender of the faith" is inevitably highstrung, nervous and unnatural. We feel an indefinable uneasiness around him, because the true weapons of the Gospel are not the harsh word and the clenched fist, but the exposed heart and the outstretched arms. We have never "fought the good fight" God's way until we have learned to love. And we cannot learn to love under all circumstances, until we have opened ourselves to learn of the One who Himself is love.

How do we learn of God? By learning of Jesus Christ. By paying interested attention to all He had to say about the Father, and to all that He did in the Father's Name. By exposing ourselves to the nature of God in Jesus Christ.

For all of His earthly life, Jesus was about His Father's

business. What was this business? Why was He sent? The Son of God came to earth so that we can, at last, know the true nature of the Father's heart.

"Lord, show us the Father and it is enough for us."

Philip voiced the heart-cry of every human being when he said this. There is no person who, if he is honest, would not admit to a longing deep inside him to know for certain what God is like.

In Jesus' answer to Philip is the answer to the heart-cry of every human life. "How long have I been with you without your recognizing Me, Philip! He who has looked on Me, has looked on the Father '

In His words and in His actions, Jesus declared Himself to be one with the Father. "I and the Father are one."

Peaceful Christians know this to be true.

They are peaceful at the center of their beings because they have seen that God cannot be figured out by the study of physics or biology; He cannot be discovered as He really is in a storm or a waterfall; He cannot be learned through a scholarship or a plan of salvation. He is in all of these, but there is more. He is a living Person, and when He broke into human history at the birth of Jesus, He involved Himself forever in the human struggle. Peaceful Christians are those who rest in the knowledge that God is discoverable to anyone. And as we discover His true character we rest.

Anyone can look at Jesus Christ. And anyone who looks at Him, looks at God Himself, or Jesus was wrong in His entire presentation of truth. A peaceful Christian sees no need to argue and defend the truth he believes. He sees only the need to witness to Jesus Christ, who declared Himself to be truth. "I am the way, the *truth,* and the life."

Throughout the Gospel accounts we see Jesus Christ in a tireless attempt to reveal the Father's heart as it is. The whole of this greatest life said to us in effect: "Look at Me. I and the Father are One. This is what God is really like. Look at Me. You need have no more doubts about His intentions toward you. I have come so that anyone can know and know fully about the Father's heart."

It seems to me that everything Jesus did had one motive behind it: To explain the Father accurately to us. The whole dynamic of His Kingdom teaching lay in the glorious fact that the King is Father.

To be able to know God is the deepest longing of every human heart. To have unanswered questions about Him is the source of all human fear. God knew this. And so He came, and now anyone can know.

Perhaps the most complete picture of the Father which Jesus gave in His earthly teachings, is His magnificently constructed prodigal son story. And most glorious to me is the fact that Jesus knew no description of God would be complete without a description of us alongside it. There is the errant prodigal in us all. There is a hard streak of the elder brother in us all. It is as though even Jesus would have had no way to express the Father as He is, without including us, as we are!

From the *Berkeley Version* I would like to quote the fifteenth chapter of Saint Luke, from verse 11 through verse 32. As you read it, check your own concept of the Father. Is He like this to you? And how much of the prodigal is there in you? How much of the elder brother?

"He further said, A certain man had two sons, the younger of whom said to his father, 'Father, give me the share of the property that is coming to me.' So he apportioned to them his means of living. After a few days the younger son collected all he had and traveled to a distant country, and there he squandered what he had in reckless living. When all had been squandered, a terrible famine visited that whole land and he began to lack; so he went and attached himself to a citizen of that country, who sent him into his fields to feed swine. He aimed to get his stomach filled with locust pods which the hogs were eating; but no one gave him any. But when he came to himself, he said, 'How many of my father's hired hands have more than they can eat and here I am starving! I will arise and go to my father and say to him, "Father, I have sinned against heaven and before you and I no longer deserve to be called your son; take me on as one of your hired hands!" '

"So he got up and went to his father; but when he was still a great way off, his father saw him and felt deeply moved (for him) and, running, fell on his neck and kissed him. The son said to him, 'Father, I have sinned against heaven and before you; I no longer deserve to be called your son!' But the father told his servants, 'Hurry! Fetch the choicest robe and put it on him; put a ring on his hand and sandals on his feet; bring the fatted calf, too, and butcher it. Let us feast and be merry; for this my son was dead and he lives again; he was lost and has been found.' So they began to be merry.

"But his older son was in the field and, as he came near home, he heard music and dancing; so, calling one of the boys, he asked what it was all about. He told him, 'Your brother has come and your father has butchered the fatted calf, because he got him back in good health.' Stirred with anger, however, he would not even go in. His father came out to invite him; but he replied to his father, 'See here! I have worked for you all these years without ever neglecting an order of yours; but never yet did you give me so much as a kid, so that I might make merry with my friends. But when this son of yours comes along after squandering your livelihood with prostitutes, you kill for him the fatted calf.' But he said to him, 'Child, you are always with me and all I have is yours. We just had to make merry and to be happy for this your brother was dead and he has come to life; he was lost and has been found.'"

"We just *had* to make merry and to be happy." Does the God you know have a capacity for merriment and rejoicing? According to Jesus Christ, this is part of the nature of the Father's heart. He is not laying down a standard for an earthly father to live up to in this little story. He is attempting once more to show us what our Heavenly Father is like. And according to Jesus, when one "lost" person comes home, truly repentant, the Father just *has* to rejoice and be happy. He can't help it. This is what He is like.

It is no wonder that this is a perfectly constructed story from a literary standpoint. It was composed by the One "by whom all things were made that were made." The Creator Himself became our Saviour, and He told this amazing story. As a writer, I find its pattern exciting to me. As a human being who desperately needs to know God's nature, its pattern also excites me. Because Jesus has with simple, clear strokes placed the characterization of God Himself *between* two characterizations of typical human nature, where it is most needed.

Actually there are three little stories here. One of the prodigal son, one of the father, and one of the elder brother.

The prodigal son story has a happy ending. In this story, Jesus deals first of all with the willful, self-centered, grasping extremities of human nature. The prodigal son wanted what was coming to him—now. He didn't want to wait. It may not show up socially in us as it did in him, but there is this grasping nature in us all. And clearly, in three simple, decisive steps Jesus (while telling the prodigal's story) shows us what true repentance means.

The father did not argue with him when he asked for his share of the inheritance. Neither does God argue with

us. In all things, He respects our free wills. The father
gave it to him and the boy "lived it up" in no time. Then,
looking around him, he saw that his life was not working.
He saw his need and admitted it. And this is the first step
in true repentance. To see our need and admit it.

If the story had stopped here, however, it would simply
have been an example of rather typical self-pity. Many
people see that they need something. Many remember
other people who "have more than they can eat" and then
they realize that they are starving. When the awakening
goes only this far, it sinks into self-pity and resentment
against life for treating them so cruelly. The reason I
know this boy was not just sorry for himself is that almost immediately, he made a decision. His repentance
was real. First, he confessed his need, and then he made
a decision to do something about it: "I will arise and go
to my father."

This is the second step in repentance. We make a decision. But a decision is only a temporary relief unless we
take the third step. The prodigal acted on his decision—
". . . he got up and went to his father."

This is the first of Jesus' three clearly drawn characterizations. Now, he shifts the scene quickly from the prodigal son to the father. "But when he was still a great way
off, his father saw him and felt deeply moved (for him)
and, *running*, fell on his neck and kissed him."

Is this what God is like?

It seems too good to be true that after a life of utter
destruction and waste God would be that glad to see one
person turn to Him in true repentance. But those of us
who have been "far off" know that it is too good *not* to
be true.

When we make one small honest move toward God, we
find Him running toward us with a warm greeting and a
kiss!

When we make one small honest move toward God,

while we are still "a great way off," we find God *running* toward us. If we see Him as He is, our repentant hearts are still more aroused toward Him, because we know He has been out looking for us. He has not been busy doing other things. The father of the prodigal had to be out on the front porch looking for him, otherwise he could not have run down the road to meet the boy coming home.

Of course, we, like the prodigal, can't help pouring out our hearts in repentance once we see Him coming toward us, but here is an interesting thing. According to Jesus' story, the father didn't say anything to the boy. He just threw his arms around him and kissed him! Any earthly father might have given the boy a good scolding at least. "Well, I could have told you! Look at you—and all my hard-earned money down the drain. To think that a son of *mine* would end up like this!"

Not the Heavenly Father. He threw his arms around the boy and kissed him and without a word to the prodigal, he began to give orders to his servants to prepare a big feast. "Hurry, fetch the choicest robe and put it on him; put a ring on his hand and sandals on his feet; bring the fatted calf, too, and butcher it. Let us feast and be merry; for this my son was dead and he lives again; he was lost and has been found."

Is God really like this? Does the mere fact of our coming to Him, even in our disgusting condition, bring joy to His heart? According to Jesus Christ, yes. And according to anyone who has dragged his wasted life home to the Father, yes.

God knows that sin in His loved ones is a disease over which they have no control. He knows the inevitable end result of a human heart thrown recklessly at life. The prodigal's father was neither surprised nor shocked at his son's condition when he came home. He just "rejoiced over him with singing." The boy had come home. To the father, that was all that mattered. God's love is greater

than our love of sin. No matter what we have done, we
can all come home and we can all hear the Father say, "I
love you more than you love your sin."

But what of the elder brothers among us? What of
those who have not "squandered what they have in reckless living"? How much does the Father love those who
stay with Him and conduct themselves uprightly? This
brings up an interesting point. As long as we feel we deserve God's love, we take it for granted. If we are not
shocking ourselves by any particular excess, it is somehow
difficult, often impossible, for us to realize the depth of
His love.

I remember, as I write, some real anger in the faces of
a few Christians who let me know shortly after my own
conversion that they resented the fact that I *felt* God's
love for me. They had known Him a long time, and like
the elder brother, they were unable to share in my feast.
They resented the ring on my hand and the robe around
my shoulders. They somehow felt that God should have
left me barefoot for awhile. After all, they had believed
and served Him for years. They deserved their sandals
and they felt slighted that the Father didn't give them
books to write and talks to make about His love. They
had been eating the whole Bread of Life for years and
they resented that for one who had been "in a far country" as I had been, He apparently had killed the fatted
calf. They were "stirred with anger and would not go in"
to my feast.

These "elder brothers" are not attractive Christians.
They are often condemned. But the Father sees them
through His eyes of love, just as He sees the prodigals
among us. He sees that neither the elder brother nor the
prodigal son are ideal people. Both are in need of a constant downpouring of divine love.

It seemed so to the elder brother, but there is really
no contrast in the way the father treated his sons. The

contrast is only in the realm of the boys' repentance. One is truly penitent, one is not. One rejoices the father's heart, one does not. But to both, he remains the entreating father. When the prodigal started home, the father "felt deeply moved (for him) and running, fell on his neck and kissed him." When the elder brother was "stirred with anger" and "would not go in," the father came out to invite him. To the prodigal he said, "Welcome home, my son." To the elder brother, "Child, you are always with me and all I have is yours."

To both he offered his heart of love and his home with all its supply.

He did not change his plans and cancel the dancing and the feasting, however, in order to pamper the surly elder brother. In all things God remains true to Himself. He merely explained that because the prodigal had returned, "We just *had* to make merry and be happy."

Is this what God is really like?

If Jesus came in order to show us once and for all what the Father is like, then it is true. During His life on earth, through His teaching and His healing and His miracles, He was motivated by one desire: to reveal the true character of God. This story of the prodigal son, the stories of the lost coin and the lost sheep are, in a sense, prologues to the Cross. As He walked the dusty roads of Palestine, Jesus said over and over, '*This* is what the Father's heart is like."

Then, on the Cross, He allowed humanity to tear open His heart, so that we can see for ourselves. God's own heart was exposed on Calvary. Because "God *was* in Christ, reconciling the world unto Himself."

# 7

# Can God Understand Our Temptations?

# 7

---

# CAN GOD UNDERSTAND OUR

# TEMPTATIONS?

We are told in the Bible that God will not allow us to be tempted more than we are capable of resisting (I Corinthians 10:13). We are told that just at the moment temptation comes to us most strongly, God will "provide a way out."

Most of us, however, find it difficult to discover the nature of this "way out." We believe that God is equal to our temptations, but *how* is He equal? How do we lay hold of His power to resist the things which so strongly attract us? More deeply than this, how do we arrive at the place of wanting to resist certain temptations?

I have personally discovered something of the nature of God's "way out" of temptation, as I have continued to discover the nature of God Himself. He does not command us to resist this or that in order to hold down our deepest desires. He commands as He does in order to release them. If we submit to Jesus Christ in one area, we ultimately find release in many other areas. But even when we have once experienced this, we still need willingness at times to want to obey Him. It is here that we must somehow see at last that He does not command from a distance. He has been in this human life Himself. "For not at all to angels did He reach out to help, but to the offspring of Abraham; so He had to be made like His brothers in every respect. . . ."

God Himself knew "He *had* to be made like His brothers in every respect." We dare not slide over this. Knowing us as He does, He knew that He could do nothing short of becoming one of us. There would be no other way we could really believe His total understanding of our human predicament. There is something of the skeptic in us all where obedience is concerned. We long to say, "Yes, but He was God. He could do it. I am a weak human being. I cannot." In one sense this is true. We must have the indwelling life of Christ within us in order to have power to take God's "way out" of temptation (see Chapter 13). But even before we come to the place of making use of His indwelling life, we often need to find the willingness to escape temptation. Indeed, at times, we need to find the "way out" itself. It is always there. We have God's word for that. But our circumstances, our heredity, our environment, our emotional disturbances, have caused us to erect such high barriers between ourselves and God, something must knock them down before our understanding can lay hold of His. Before we are willing even to discuss our deepest needs, we must know that the other person understands.

God does understand human temptation. He understood it before He broke into human history in the Person of Jesus. But He understood it so well that He knew we would be tempted to believe that He does not understand!

This lack of trust in God's ability to identify with us in all of our weaknesses is consciously or unconsciously behind every human struggle. We have allowed our very reverence for Him, our very realization of His holiness, of

His power, to come between us and God. Unless we have dared to believe that God allowed Himself to be born into the human race, we keep Him so "high and lifted up" that we lose all hope of contact with Him in certain areas where our human temptations plague us.

Surely, He is a Holy God, "high and lifted up." This we need to know before the fact of His visit to this earth in human form takes on the dynamic it must have for us. We need the background of the majestic, powerful God of the Old Testament. We need to be startled into the realization that this same God confined Himself to a human body. This realization is what begins to crush our barriers to His understanding of the earth-pulls of a daily human life.

Once we see that the "high and lifted up" Holy One of Israel stripped Himself of everything but His God-heart for our sakes, we can do nothing but go to Him!

If I did not believe in the Deity of Jesus Christ, I would not be a Christian. If I still believed Jesus of Nazareth to be merely one more Great Teacher, I would still be struggling along my dead-end road, vainly trying to fit His thinking into the pattern of several other great teachers in human history and mine into theirs. I know now that although He became utterly human, He also remained God. I tried, but could not accept the theory held by some that Jesus kept in such strict obedience and close contact with the Father that He *became* divine. Jesus Christ *was* in the beginning, and "without Him was not anything made that was made."

He was the Word "with God, and the Word was God."

But He did become utterly human. "Ours is not a High Priest who cannot sympathize with our weaknesses, but One who was in every respect tempted as we have been —but without sin." He did not yield to temptation, but Jesus Christ *was* tempted—"in every respect as we have been."

A recent religious magazine article declared that the temptations of Jesus could not have been of the same earthly nature as ours. This leaves me cold. This robs His coming of much of its meaning. This is not what the Bible declares to be true.

In all other religions man is reaching for God. Trying to attain Him. If I believed this were possible, I should probably be following another religion. I am a Christian because I see my own helplessness to reach God. I am a Christian because I now see clearly my own need to be lifted up. I am a Christian because I know that He reached down to me in Jesus Christ. And in order to get my attention and my confidence, "He had to be made like his brothers in every respect." He knew this was the only way I would not be afraid to look at Him openly and talk to Him honestly from my heart. He knew that if He had not come down here and entered the human struggle, something in us would always be a little afraid of looking up into His face as He sits on what seems to us a dazzling and almost frighteningly distant throne.

I once heard His coming explained this way: Jesus of Nazareth is God's transformer. Before electricity can be of any use in a cottage or a skyscraper, it must pass through a transformer. Before it does, it is too powerful. The cottage and the office building would remain dark if it were not for the transformer, which brings the electrical power down to a place where it is useful in a light bulb.

Jesus Christ brought God down to us; to the realm of our daily lives. He did not diminish God, He merely brought Him to us. We can grasp the character and the intentions of another human being. In Jesus, we can grasp God's character and intentions. In Jesus, anyone can know what God is like. No one human being can ever grasp all that Jesus tells us of the Father, but anyone can discover for himself that for all eternity we will never find one single contradiction among the members of the

Godhead. The heart of the Father is the same as the heart of the Son, and the same heart motivates the Holy Spirit, who is simply God with us and in us now.

James Crichton, the Scottish scholar and adventurer, once wrote: "The death of Christ is a great mystery; but His birth is even a greater. That He should live a human life at all is stranger than that, so living, He should die a human death. I can scarce get past His cradle in my wondering, to wonder at His cross. The infant Jesus is, in some views, a greater marvel than Jesus with the purple robe and the crown of thorns."

That "He had to be made like His brothers in every respect," is God's great gesture of love toward us.

He created us and He understands more about the workings of our minds and our emotions than any other living person. He, being God, and having His own holiness with which to contrast it, understands more about the shackling power of sin and the downpull of temptation than any other living person. He knows that we cannot, in our own strength, rise above it.

And knowing this, He did what He had to do. He came down to us. He has been in it, too. Through His Holy Spirit, He is still in it with us. He knows. He not only knows because He is God, He knows because He has experienced human life. We have already said that from His side He did not need to experience it in order to know it, but He knew that from *our* side He did. If He had not come, He knew that we would forever try to hide from Him, secretly despairing of ever knowing Him in the strictly personal way He longs for us to know Him.

In the next four chapters I want to share some of what His humanity has come to mean to me. Those among us who call ourselves evangelical Christians tend to miss much of what seems to me to be one of the major motivations of God's visit to this earth. We do not dwell enough on His humanity. Perhaps some are afraid of being called "liberal." I am no longer afraid of being called anything except "unliberal" in the love department. And my capacity to love has been steadily increased as I have seen more and more of *why* God chose to become a human being.

God not only understands our temptations, He can discuss them with us. And we can feel free to discuss them with Him. "For ours is not a High Priest who cannot sympathize with our weaknesses, but One who was in every respect tempted as we have been. . . . For not at all to angels did He reach out to help, but to the offspring of Abraham; so He had to be made like His brothers in every respect. . . ."

Fully realizing our plight, God saw what He had to do.

# 8

# Was Christ Tempted by
# Hungers Like Ours?

# 8

---

## WAS CHRIST TEMPTED BY

## HUNGERS LIKE OURS?

Sometime during the first few weeks of my Christian life I heard a radio sermon by a Scottish minister. Most of what he said I didn't understand at all. Not that his brogue was too thick. It was just right, and his diction was beautiful. Most of what he said sailed past me because I had not heard sermons in my adult life and the "language of Zion" was almost as unintelligible to me as a foreign language. But he did repeat one phrase which I shall never forget and which even I, with my utter lack of doctrinal background, could grasp easily.

His phrase struck my heart for two reasons. First, because his brogue reminded me of my own Scottish Grandfather who recited Lord Byron and Robert Burns to me when I was a child. But its impact on my heart was deeper than this. His repeated phrase, I realize now, was what my heart had longed so to hear. The preacher sounded like my Grandfather, but he wasn't quoting "The Cotter's Saturday Night"; he was declaring warmly, over and over, that "Ther-r's a Mon on the thr-rone up ther-re! Ther-r's a *Mon* on the thr-rone up ther-re!"

63

Now, ten years later, I know as I've never known before that there is a Man on the throne up there. A Man-God walked the earth when Jesus walked. A Man-God went to the Cross. A Man-God left the tomb and returned to His Father. And the "lamb in the midst of the throne" *now* is still a Man-God. My heart opens to Him more and more as I realize that this Man remembers to this day what it feels like to be a human being. He has not forgotten in the midst of the joyful return to heavenly places. The bright angel bands who attend Him do not take His mind off the earth for one instant. The music of heaven does not make Him deaf to our cries. No celestial light blinds Him to our sorrow. No feast in paradise will ever make Him forget our hungers.

We have already seen that the Bible tells us He "was in every respect tempted as we have been." If we believe that God and Jesus Christ are one and the same, then we know that God understands hunger of all kinds.

Basic hunger of one kind or another is at the source of every temptation. When we yield to our own desires to attempt to satisfy our various basic hungers in our own way, we sin. Self-pity, which is sin, springs from a hunger for something which we don't have and which we feel life should give us. Self-pity can and has driven men to murder.

A recent newspaper account told of a man who had lost his wife to another man. At first, he tried to adjust to his loneliness without the woman he loved. But his "hunger" for her companionship, her presence in the empty house, was too much for him. He made many visits to a psychiatrist in an effort to recover from his confessed self-pity over his continuing longing for his wife. Instead, his hunger turned to hatred for the other man. In a blind rage one night he drove to the man's store, whipped out a gun and shot him. Then he turned the same gun on himself. The inherent bent toward sin in human nature had overpowered him. What began with the perfectly normal desire of a man for his wife turned, in the time of stress over losing her, into murder and suicide.

Basic hunger in men and women, if it is not fulfilled in a creative way, is the cause of excessive drinking.

A man whom I had known for several years returned from the service after World War II to find his wife in love with someone else. My friend had never had a home of his own. He had been supporting himself, with both parents dead, since the age of twelve. The girl he married in haste just before going overseas symbolized more than a wife. She stood for the one bright security which had held him during his long months of battle service—a home of his own. When she was gone, he tried to escape from his excruciating pain with one bottle after another. But at last someone got to this man with the good news about God. It has taken more than eight years, but now he is no longer drinking. He is married again, has a home and family, a good job, and he will tell you enthusiastically that Jesus Christ understood his hunger.

Christ did not condemn this man for drinking. He saved him from it. It took a long time. Somehow it does take a long time for some of us to realize that God is not shocked; that He understands these things. And while He cannot approve of anything that damages His loved ones, as sin surely does, He waits with His arms outstretched toward us, until we stop fighting His imagined remoteness and recognize His complete willingness.

I once heard it said that heaven is the place where man says to God, "Thy will be done." And hell is the place where God reluctantly says to man, "Thy will be done." I know of nothing outside of God's love as wide as His willingness to reach to us.

I spoke not long ago with a woman who was suffering real hunger. Not physically; as with most of us, she had all her physical needs met. Hers was a particular kind of searing intellectual hunger. She loved her husband, but intellectually they were incompatible. His interest in literature was completely satisfied by the financial and sports pages of the daily newspaper. Her love of good books was insatiable. He hated concerts. She loved them. She painted rather well and he laughed at her efforts. But his laughter didn't bother her as it once had. She had, in the main, accepted her husband as being the non-intellectual, but kind, hardworking and honest man he was. She had even learned to insert football into her schedule of things to watch on TV. Her problem was not so much a complaint about her husband as he was, but an honest intellectual hunger to be able to share some of the things she loved with another human being whom she loved.

Her hungering heart seemed to be encouraged as she began to see that the Lord had Himself experienced agonizing, basic hunger when He was on earth. In a deeper way He was able to enter her life when she became convinced that He did not condemn her honest hunger, but understood it.

It is obvious that the teen-ager who becomes a delinquent is driven by a basic hunger to be wanted and noticed. To be important. If we face facts, we see that hunger of some kind motivates every uncontrolled, sin-crippled human personality.

I have found great help in a careful examination of Jesus' temptations in the wilderness. Not from the standpoint at first of how to resist temptation, but from the fact that not once during His earthly life did He try to protect His humanity. As I see this, I find myself more willing to take His promised strength in order to resist temptation in my life.

Jesus Christ was all that could be contained of God in a human being. He could have protected His humanity, but He did not. And the realization that He did not,

melts my heart into a new willingness to obey. The melt-
ing of our hearts by love is God's way of getting at us.
We, of course, must expose our hearts to His. But as I
see that Jesus on the Cross is God Himself exposing His
heart to me, I find myself willing to open mine to Him.
And the *why* of His visit to the earth takes on a new
meaning.

In Luke's account of the wilderness temptations of
Jesus (chapter 4:1-13) the Lord was tempted first to
satisfy His own physical hunger. And according to verse
two, He *was* tempted. Anyone who has ever dieted knows
a little of what hunger can do to our personalities. Perhaps some who read this book may have known periods
of real hunger. At any rate, physical hunger can cause
havoc in many areas of the total person other than our
bodies.

It is of the utmost importance here that we remember
Jesus was not only the Son of God, He was a human being, too. A Man with a digestive and emotional system
like ours. He did not have some special dispensation
which made His hunger-pains of a gentle, ethereal nature.
He was suffering intensely, in the wilderness, both physically and emotionally. Food is definitely tied up with our
emotions. So, His sufferings had to be emotional as well
as physical.

He was starving, but He did not turn the stones into
bread, as the tempter invited Him to do. Because He was
One with God, and because "without him was not anything made that was made," He could have done it. He
created the stones in the first place and He also created
the wheat for the bread. Nothing more than a momentary
re-creation would have been involved in turning those
stones to bread as Jesus stood there in the wilderness
alone and hungry. The fact that He could have done it
does not amaze me. The amazing thing to me is that He
did not do it!

If we look at Him closely as He really is, we see that He could not have done it without sinning against His own nature. "God is love." He doesn't merely have a loving heart, He *is* love. And if He had satisfied His own physical and emotional hunger that day in the agony of that wilderness hour, what emotionally or physically hungry man or woman down through the ages would have listened to Him?

He was thinking, during those hours of His own intense hunger, of every other hungry person who would ever live. Because I see this, I can now speak quietly and confidently about Jesus Christ to a mother whose child has just died of leukemia. I don't need to have shared her particular hunger. I can remind her that He shared a kind of hunger that day which gives Him access to every hungry human heart. I can speak about Jesus Christ with great certainty to the woman who has just been deserted by her husband and whose emotions are at the starvation point. I can assure her that Jesus knows. And because I can assure her of this fact, her heart can then bear to open toward Him and to believe that He will, in His way, fulfill that hunger.

The fact that Jesus Christ is God and has a right to make claims upon our lives is not enough to open a heart bruised and swollen shut with suffering. And He knew this. To point to God's rights often only hardens our hearts. We don't mean for it to happen, but a demand (even if it comes from God) upon a heart already battered by suffering, causes us to throw up still another defense around it. Still another layer of protection.

Seeing that Jesus Christ did not once protect His own humanity not only melts my own heart into more willingness to obey, it has made witnessing to other persons increasingly simple. I am no longer trying to "sell" anyone on God. I am merely allowing God to show me first that He has already done all that is required to handle all conditions of all human hearts in Jesus Christ. Then I can quietly pass on my certainty.

Whatever the outward or inward hungers of the human heart, the basic hunger in all humanity is to know God. Jesus Christ has not only experienced hunger for you, He offers Himself to satisfy that one basic hunger to know God.

Humanity cries: "Lord, give us this bread all the time!"

Jesus replies: "I am the Bread of life. He who comes to Me will never starve and he who believes in Me shall not suffer thirst anymore."

# 9

## Was He Tempted by Ambition?

# 9

---

## WAS HE TEMPTED BY AMBITION?

We have already looked at some of the unfolding wonder of the fact that not once did Jesus Christ protect His own humanity when He walked the earth as God. He could have, but He did not.

His heart, knowing our hearts, would not permit it.

He loved the entire world so much that He gave Himself for it. How would He have dared commit one act of self-protection which might have shut out even one person?

In Chapter 7, we shared from Luke 4:1-4 Jesus' first temptation in the wilderness. Had He turned even one small stone into a loaf of bread, He would have shut Himself off from all the hungry people in the world. And I believe His love is so great that if only one person in all the ages was going to know hunger of any kind, He still would not have fed Himself that day.

To me, it is not enough to say that Jesus Christ was sinless because He was the Son of God. I must press further and know that He was the Son of God because He was sinless. He was a human being, but He thought with God's mind and loved with God's heart.

This lifts my allegiance to Him out of the mere dogma

73

of doctrine and gives it heart and conviction. As I see that God's true character is discoverable in Jesus Christ, my inherent resistance toward Him melts away. I do not need to whip myself up into loyalty to Him. My intellect itself, enlightened by His Holy Spirit, demands that I follow Him. My heart cries, "God *has* to be like Jesus!" Life will not be justified otherwise.

In one sense, the authentic Christian who believes in Jesus Christ as the revelation of God Himself is the only one who truly believes in human dignity! Humanism, as a philosophy, falls far short here. When I see in Christ how important man is to God, I can only conclude that "all else is vanity" but to belong to Him.

If only one person in all the world had needed a Saviour, He would still have gone to the Cross.

This *knowing* opens hearts. Opens hearts to receive Him as Saviour and opens hearts to follow Him as Lord.

To know Jesus Christ as Lord and God as Thomas knew Him, is, in the philosophical sense, to know a self-evident truth. When we link our lives to His, we find that He Himself is His own verifiable data.

Across the nearly two thousand years of the history of Christianity on earth, men have tried to kill off in themselves ambition, or the human bent to self-glorification. This has become a fetish in many religious groups. Men have often injured themselves physically in their desperate efforts to become humble, to choke off their naturally ambitious natures. To some Christian groups, both Catholic and Protestant, this has been the indication, if not the way, to what man calls salvation.

The Protestant may believe that his salvation comes only as a result of faith in God, but over and over he has attempted to prove his salvation, to man at least, by appearing to be humble. By running himself down in order to "glorify God." By setting up a man-concocted list of do's and don'ts and forcing himself and the others in his group to follow them.

Somewhere throughout all of Christian history, there have been and still are those who attempt to erect boundaries around the Christian life. To "fence in" what Christ came to set free! André Gide referred to the "cramp of salvation." Before I met Jesus Christ and knew Him to be God Himself, I looked with horror on the possibility of confining my life to what I honestly believed to be the boxed-in existence of the followers of Christ. Now that I have been His follower for ten years, I see that this is not His way. It has been the way of those who try sincerely to work out their own guilt feelings by self-effort, in an admirable but futile manner. Doctrinally, they may believe that Christ on His Cross handled the guilt of all human nature. Experientially, they work at squelching themselves until their daily lives do indicate a state of spiritual "cramp."

When we put ourselves in a box, we follow what Dr. J. B. Phillips calls a "God-in-a-box." In his great Christian classic, *Your God Is Too Small*, Dr. Phillips says: "The man who is outside all organized Christianity may have, and often does have, a certain reverence for God, and a certain genuine respect for Jesus Christ. But what sticks in his throat about the Christianity of the Churches is not merely their differences in denomination, but the spirit of 'churchiness' which seems to pervade them all. They seem to him to have captured and tamed and trained to their own liking Something that is really far too big ever to be forced into little man-made boxes with neat labels upon them. 'If,' the Churches appear to be saying to him, 'you will jump through our particular hoop or sign on our particular dotted line then we will introduce you to God. But if not, then there is no God for you.' This seems to him to be nonsense, and nasty arrogant nonsense at that. 'If there's a God at all,' he feels rather angrily, 'then He's here in the home and in the street, here in the pub and in the workshop. And if it's true that He's interested in me and wants me to love and serve Him, then He's available for me and every other Tom, Dick or Harry who wants Him, without any interference from the professionals. If God is God, He's big, and generous and magnificent, and I can't see that anybody can say they've made a particular corner on God, or shut Him up in their particular box.' " [1]

These are strong words, and written by a clergyman, too. Of course, as Dr. Phillips elaborates, we see that no one group intends to do this. And neither do I believe we can attack them outwardly and leave it at that. Attacks avail nothing anyway. And they are not necessary at all. What is necessary is for us to look at God as we can see Him in Jesus Christ and discover individually that no matter what Christendom has done through the years since His resurrection, to make itself appear "separate" or right or humble or "saved," Christ can still give us the straight word on self-gratification or ambition and make us realistic about it.

If you, as an outsider, are cringing at the thought that if you become a Christian you will have to douse the ambition that possesses you and crawl into the "box" with the others you know, forget it.

God may not approve of your particular ambition, or He may need to change you so that it no longer possesses you, but He does understand it. And He will redirect it for you—creatively.

Going on with our inspection of Jesus' temptations in the wilderness, we see that in the second temptation (Luke 4:5-8) He makes possible the opening of the hearts of the overly ambitious. Here He was shown the kingdoms of the world and told that He could rule over them. In verses one and two of Chapter 4, remember that He "was led by the Spirit into the wilderness, being forty days *tempted*."

Jesus was tempted.

It is no effort for me to resist robbing a bank when I pass one. I'm just not tempted to do it. This is no virtue on my part. Merely lack of interest. In order to be tempted we need the desire within us to do or have a thing. Something in us must respond to it. This is why a feeling of pride in a Christian because he doesn't drink —when he has never wanted to—is ridiculous!

But Jesus Christ, unlike many religious groups, does not approach your temptation to further yourself, by shutting you in a box. He approaches it, as He approaches your total personality, out in the open with all of Himself. He became a human being. He remained God, but He was also utterly human. Something in Him responded to ruling the kingdoms of the world. He was tempted. He approaches you realistically and with full freedom on your part and His. He does not attempt to get you to pour yourself into an accepted mold in order to appear pious, or unambitious, or humble, or "saved."

He approaches you as you are with Himself, as He is. He lets you know that He not only understands your ambition to get to the top quickly, He lets you know that He was tempted on this point, too! This fact in itself makes me more willing to be honest with Him concerning my own temptations along the lines of ambition. Before I became His follower, I was driven by ambition to reach the top in my profession. Since I have known Him, this is still one of my strongest temptations. Now and then I receive an offer to write something which I know is either not God's highest will for my life or which is against His will. But it may further my career as a writer.

What can I do here?

Use my will power and turn it down? Yes, I can. But there are two dangers involved in this. There is, first of all, the danger that in turning it down I am pushing down into my subconscious mind the beginnings of a resentment against God for having a will like His instead of a will like mine. And there is always present the danger of becoming "spiritually ambitious" because I feel pride in having turned it down for His sake!

God does not pour us in a mold. He has said: "Come now, and let us reason together." And this is the Christian way. The Christian who has taken the time to find out what God is really like in Jesus Christ can go right to Him no matter what the temptation. We do not need to have come to the final decision before telling Him about it. Even if we are still fighting in our hearts, we are perfectly free to confront Him with, "But, Lord, how can You possibly know or understand how I feel in this particular situation? After all, You're 'meek and lowly in heart.' I'm ambitious! Ambition didn't bother You. But it bothers me. What can You say to me directly on this, Lord?"

And He can reply, "I know exactly how you feel. Don't forget, I was tempted there in the wilderness that day. I was tempted with the offer of those earthly kingdoms. I do know how you feel. I knew that earthly kingdoms were not what I really wanted in the end. Being one with the Father, I knew that all that would ultimately satisfy Me would be the hearts of the people who made up these kingdoms. I knew this to be the Father's highest will, and so it was Mine, too. Even if you can't see this right now, you can trust Me to know best. And I have opened the way for your obedience by the very fact that I allowed Myself to be tempted along this same line. Follow Me!"

In this same temptation, He also has a direct word for the nobodies among us. Jesus identified totally with the little people of this world, all the way from His birth in the most humiliating surroundings, to His death on a criminal's cross. And He did not forget the nobodies among us that day in the wilderness when He turned down the kingdoms of this world.

Most people are never offered a kingdom on this earth. Most people just go along making ends meet. Now, suppose Jesus Christ had yielded to the temptation to become an earthly ruler. Suppose He had accepted just one tiny kingdom! Could a nobody even want to come close to a God like that? Could the average person feel that he or she had a right to come close and ask of a God like that?

Jesus Christ lays down no complicated rules. His great commandment is that we love the Lord our God with all our hearts. In His every action, He showed that He knew we could never do this until we knew what God was like. And so, in His every action, He showed us the heart of God. The only heart magnetic enough to draw us away from self-love and personal ambition.

He showed us the Father when He showed us Himself. He dared to say, "I, if I be lifted up . . . will draw all men." And He dared to say it because He knew who He was! His is not a static, cramped plan of salvation. His is the eternal offer of a strictly personal relationship with Himself, in which we can know we are understood, and through which our every temptation can be met. His offer is not a life lived in a box of religious platitudes and rules. It is a life lived in the open wonder of an ever brightening personal relationship with Himself.

Anyone can talk things over with God through Jesus Christ and come to a creative conclusion. In these wilderness temptations and on through His earthly life, to the Cross and the open tomb, He has made nearness to Himself possible for every type of human being. Not only has He made it possible, He has made it irresistible, once we know Him as He is.

# 10

# Was He Tempted to Prove Himself?

# 10

---

## WAS HE TEMPTED TO PROVE HIMSELF?

Perhaps the most difficult thing for anyone is to be willing to be misunderstood.

Something within every human being longs for at least one other person to know why we are as we are. To know why we do what we do. To know why we think as we think. True, many of us may not know our real motives ourselves, but as far as we know, we want to be sure someone else sees us as we at least think we are.

If we are right or innocent, it is a frantic experience to know that no one believes us to be right or innocent. Such a sense of frustration is set up in us that we long to do something startling to prove our point or our position.

A college girl once said to me, "Sometimes when I can't convince my mother that I didn't do what she insists I did, I want to beat my head against her head to prove it!" I am not quite clear how the young lady thought this would prove her point, but I can certainly understand her helpless dilemma. There is that in us that makes us frantic until someone believes us. Especially if it matters a great deal to us.

It is no secret that this exceedingly human trait is at the bottom of many heated religious arguments. This is perhaps an extreme example, but unfortunately it is not an isolated one. When I was a new Christian, I sat in on a discussion between one brother who held the Calvinist view of eternal security, and another who held the Arminian view. I confess now that although I had known Christ for almost two years, it so happened that I hadn't understood the difference between the two views until that day. In fact, both terms were still quite vague to me. But because of my ignorance, I merely listened and in no time I caught on that the Calvinist brother knew he would never lose his "salvation." Further listening showed me that the Arminian brother believed that if he slipped from his concept of the straight and narrow, he would. One of them (and I honestly can't remember now which one it was) finally grew so exasperated in his frantic desire to prove his point that he shouted, "So help me, brother, if I thought it would knock you out of your darkness, I'd hit you over the head with this book-end!"

This is not the place to argue either side of the eternal security question. I have never seen the necessity for that anyway. Jesus Christ is my security, and He has said, "Lo, I am with you always." I simply believe Him and let it go at that. Salvation is His business, not mine. But my point is clear, I am sure. Both brothers were gripped by that frantic seizure from within to have someone agree with us. To be recognized as being right. Right here it might be well to say that true humility is not the need to be proven right on a point. It is the willingness to be made right in our hearts. And Jesus Christ, so far as I know, was the only perfectly humble Man who has ever walked this earth. "Learn of me, for I am meek and lowly in heart." He was.

But He did become a human being, and in the third temptation in the wilderness, according to the Gospel of

Luke (chapter 4:9-13) we find Him tempted, humanly speaking, to prove Himself.

The account says that He was invited by the tempter to cast Himself down from a pinnacle of the Temple in order to prove (as it was written) that the angels would protect Him from harm.

Alone, weary, hungry and knowing the hard work that lay ahead if He fulfilled His Father's mission on earth, Jesus heard this proposition: "If you are God's Son, throw yourself down from here, for it is written, 'He will give orders to His angels on your behalf to protect you,' and 'They shall carry you on their hands so that you may not stub your foot against a stone.' "

There He stood (on the "summit of the temple") and there before Him was a sensational opportunity to prove His identity. He knew how slow would be man's heart to accept Him as the Messiah. Knowing human nature as He did, He knew that if He jumped from that "summit of the temple," literally thousands would believe He was who He claimed to be. After all, He knew the Old Testament Scripture to which the tempter referred. Jesus was well trained in the Scriptures. He knew Psalm 91:11 declared that the angels of the Lord would protect Him, because He knew He was the Son of God.

If he jumped and landed safely, wouldn't this be proof that He was who He claimed to be? The public will always go for the sensational. Could any other person on earth jump so far and not be injured? He could, but again, He did not.

Just one more instance of the fact that in no way did Jesus Christ ever protect His humanity. He did nothing to save Himself which we cannot do to save ourselves. He became one with us, even as He remained one with the Father. But because He remained one with the Father, He did nothing extravagant to win men's hearts. He used no sensational means to collect a following. He did nothing superficial to point to Himself. He was tempted to jump. The Bible says He was. But He didn't, and so He can say to the whole of frantic, misunderstood human nature, "I know how you feel. I've been through it, too. Learn of me."

No one finds "rest unto his soul" by displaying himself, or by using drastic measures to prove his point. If Jesus had in any way sanctioned human exhibitionism, I quake to think of what some religious workers might be doing now. If we resort to one bit of sensationalism or force to prove our points, we are then only faced with finding something a little more sensational or a little more forceful in order to keep things going. Jesus knew this about human nature. He thought up the human mind and He thought up the universe into which He placed it. He knows exactly what works out and what does not. He did not restrain Himself from jumping merely in order to obey the Father's will. He knew that the Father's will contained nothing quixotic or tricky or sensational. He knew that the Father's will contained no desire for the superficial "belief" which would follow an amazing "stunt," and then quickly fade away. He knew the Father longed to get at the very hearts of men.

I am well aware from having been out there just ten years ago, that those who do not follow Christ have genuine grounds for confusion as Christians spend themselves in heated and futile blasts at one another, each group attempting to prove itself right.

But for you who are not yet believers in Christ, I beg of you to remember that the Lord Himself did not resort to such superficial, unheavenly means. You are not being called to follow other Christians, you are being called by Jesus Christ to follow Him. And it is well to remember also that there has never yet been a follower of Christ who has become completely like Him.

I agree to the tragedy of the niggling differences in

Christendom. I abhor it, too. So does Christ. But don't allow niggling Christendom to keep you from the holy adventure of Christianity.

Christianity is Christ.

And in Him is no contradiction. "By Him all things were created in heaven and in earth, the visible and the invisible, whether thrones or lordships or rulers or authorities, they were all created by Him and for Him, and He is Himself before all, and *in Him all things are fitly framed together.*"

If you will go beyond Christendom to Christ Himself, you will see that "in Him all things *are* framed together." His *has* to be a heart of all-inclusive love in order to fitly frame together the warring factions of Christendom, each attempting to prove itself right.

He has enabled me to go peaceably from group to group *only* because He was able to get through to me that "everything I have, I have been given." I dare see nothing but "Jesus Christ and Him crucified." When I look away from Him, I too can fall, like you who are still outside, into utter confusion. But I need not look away from Him. And any time you are willing, you may begin to look at Him too and never again need to turn your eyes away.

Jesus Christ offered no tricks, no complicated theological plans, no sensational proofs of His identity. He offered Himself. We either accept Him or we reject Him. He could do it no other way and allow us to remain morally responsible individuals. Some may argue that His miracles and healings were "proofs." I do not think they were. To me they are merely evidences of His nature. In every instance, including the water turned to wine at Cana, His miracles were for the benefit of humanity. Not once did He employ His Deity to protect Himself. Not once did He employ His Deity in order to prove Himself. He simply went about presenting Himself to us.

Jesus did not jump from the pinnacle of the Temple. Instead He allowed Himself to be nailed to a tree. If He had jumped, a few thousand living then in Palestine would have been impressed. From the Cross He is able to call so loudly to the whole human race that even now you and I can hear.

And the choice remains ours.

# 11

## Does God Understand About Human Suffering?

# 11

## DOES GOD UNDERSTAND ABOUT HUMAN SUFFERING?

If I declare that God does understand about the suffering of His loved ones, someone will lash back with the question which has been hurled angrily toward heaven since the beginning of human suffering: "If God understands, why doesn't He do something about it?"

God does understand about the suffering of His loved ones. And His loved ones are not limited to those who openly follow Him. "For God so loved the *world* that He gave His only begotten Son." In no way is His love limited to those who have seen their need of a Saviour. If you are not a follower of Jesus Christ, His concern over the suffering in your life is just as great as is His concern over the suffering in my life. But because the Christian life is a strictly personal matter, you, by your unbelief, are blocking Him where your suffering is concerned. Just as you are blocking Him where eternal life is concerned.

God does not wave a magic wand over the head of anyone, either in the matter of eternal life or the healing of a human heart. Once and for all we must forget about cut and dried static processes. Once and for all, we must begin to see that the Christian life is a life lived person-to-Person with Jesus Christ. Together you and God work out the problems which come to you. Christians do not automatically become cosmic pets. And Christians who attempt to turn God into a cosmic errand boy, whose only work is to protect them from human suffering, have not seen the God of Calvary.

Just because you have always considered yourself a "believer," or because you have always gone to church; just because you "went forward" in a meeting, or gave yourself to Christ in the privacy of your own room, does not mean you have learned how to take His way for you in your times of suffering.

Jesus Christ declared Himself to be the way, and we learn His answers to our heart's need only by taking an active part in this person-to-Person relationship with Him. If we live the days of our lives ignoring Christ, except when we need to be protected from some sudden danger, we will find Him hard to contact when tragedy strikes. Not that He won't be there. He will be. But we will find ourselves so insensitive to His presence that it will seem to us as though He has hidden Himself from us. It is the human heart's way to jump to the conclusion that God has hidden Himself, when the truth is it is we who have thrown up the barricade from our side.

We ignore Him for so long at a time that we find ourselves suddenly unable to make contact with Him.

I recently spoke with a successful woman executive who said, "Oh, I've always prayed. When I was a child I used to pray that God wouldn't let my mother spank me when I got home late. And to this day, even when I start down a long flight of steps, I ask God to keep me from falling."

It was no amazement to me that this woman was, at the moment of our conversation, almost frantic with fear and worry over a difficult situation in her life. Her spasmodic contacts with God had been little more than superstitious cries for help. This was no constant person-to-Person relationship. If there was no one else around, and if she felt inadequate, or wanted to avoid something painful, then she sent up a little trial balloon toward heaven.

God does understand and He does act in our behalf when human suffering slashes across our hearts, but before He can act He needs our cooperation. He cannot merely shove us out of the way of pain. He would be a fiend if He pampered us in that way. Nothing destroys human character more than pampering. God's way is the way of character-building. His behavior toward us during our times of heartache goes so far beyond the too common concept of the "comforting Father with a long white beard," that such an idea of God is blasphemy!

God does understand and He longs to act in our human suffering, but He cannot do it if He does not have our attention as well as our allegiance.

Our part is, first of all, to link our lives with His. To open all we know of ourselves to all we know of Jesus Christ. The Bible says, "Believe on the Lord Jesus Christ, and thou shalt be saved." We will go into this in more detail in a later chapter, but believing in Christ simply means that you rest your entire case with Him. And if we know that He is one with God, who else is more capable of handling our cases?

I am well aware, however, that to most people this is a strange procedure. And it is strange because God is a stranger to them. If there is one point which I long to make clear in this book, it is the necessity for every human being to discover for himself what God is really like! Contained in this discovery is the potential of everyone's understanding of how to allow God to take over in time of suffering.

Few among us would approach a mere stranger on the

street and pour out our hearts to him. We trust people with our deepest needs only after we get to know them well. By this I do not mean to imply that it requires many years to know Jesus Christ. It is true, the longer we know Him, the more easily we trust Him, but when we determine to find out about the true character of God, we have Jesus' own promise that the Holy Spirit will teach us. In fact, no one can learn of God without the inner enlightenment of the Holy Spirit of God. This Spirit invades our lives when we receive Christ, and we are from then on able to make discoveries about God which those who do not believe cannot make, no matter how intellectually agile they may be. "The Spirit of Truth . . . will guide you into every truth."

As we learn of God's true character, we are able to open ourselves, even in the midst of suffering, to the loving action He longs to take in our behalf.

The writing of this chapter has been interrupted by a telephone call from a man whom I had never seen, but whose voice betrayed so much suffering my heart was immediately involved in our conversation. For two years, since his release from prison, he has lost one job after another. As soon as his employer discovers his prison record (even though his slate has been clear since then) the little pink discharge slip appears in his pay envelope. The man has a Christian background. But as he talked to me by telephone, hoping I would have a lead on a job, he was not interested in religion. He was bitter toward God, although he seemed to have no question about His existence.

My heart sagged with the weight of his trouble and leaped with joy all at once. I think it is quite evident why my heart was heavy. His was a tragic story. But there was the joy element, too. Right there as I spoke with this gentleman, the contents of this book were being proved to me all over again! I could see that he didn't know what

God is really like at all. He "believed" that Jesus Christ is God's Son, but it had no practical meaning on this icy cold Chicago day when he was suffering not only the pangs of actual physical hunger, but the agony of the heart well known to any man who longs to support his family and is frustrated at every turn.

This man felt that God had turned His back on him. I can still hear the hard-edged masculine voice, struggling to hold back tears of despair, "What else can a man think? I'm not asking anything of God except what any man has a right to ask—a chance to earn a living. If He hasn't turned His back on me, then He must be standing there laughing at me!"

Theological talk is of little value to a man with a pain in his stomach from not having eaten for two days. It is less valuable to a man with a pain in his heart because he cannot provide for his family. But I know, now and forever, that in the heart of every human being Jesus Christ has an ally. And as I discover more and more about the nature of God through my life with Christ, I become more boldly confident that He meant what He said about drawing all men unto Himself. I did not speak of a "plan of salvation" to this hungry, worried man on the telephone. I asked if he minded one personal question before we began to talk about job possibilities. He agreed, and this was my question: "Do you believe that the young Man hanging on the Cross was God Himself?"

He wasn't expecting a question like this to be called a personal question. There was a moment's silence, and when he spoke again, the hard edge in his voice was gone. "Yeah. Yeah, I guess I'd be a fool if I didn't. But what's so personal about that?"

"It's a strictly personal question, sir," I replied. "And it has directly to do with you as you stand there in that telephone booth talking to me. If that was God Himself on that Cross with His arms stretched out toward the whole world, do you think there is a remote possibility that this same God could not care about you right now?"

Little by little we began to speak of Jesus Christ Himself. The man had heard a lot of sermons, he knew some of the great Christian leaders, but he had never begun to respond to Christ in a personal way. We still haven't found a job for him, but we have some leads. And this man, who dragged himself from his bed hating life this morning, will go to sleep tonight, peaceful in the midst of his still unsolved problems.

In prayer with a friend of mine in a Chicago Loop office, he placed his case in the hands of the One who not only understands, but who now has the freedom to begin to act in the man's behalf. It is far better that his life was committed to Christ before a human solution to his work problem came about. He can know now that God Himself is deeply involved with him in all ways. In some instances, I am sure the prison record was the reason he lost his jobs. But I am also sure that a man with a chip on his shoulder against life is not a good risk as an employee. This man will need to "grow in the knowledge of the Lord Jesus Christ," but as he grows, he will find it steadily easier to rest his case with Him. The more we know about Him, the more we trust Him. Even in the midst of our suffering.

The scope of human suffering is so wide it would be impossible ever to show in detail how God acts in our behalf in each particular kind of suffering. But in all, He acts always on one basic principle—identification with us in the suffering. Jesus Christ Himself is the Supreme Sufferer. In all our pain, we find God's way through it, if we allow Christ to meet us *in it*. He does not ask that we enter into a personal relationship with some distant formless God. He became one of us, so that we can drop our defenses against Him when our hearts are breaking. His heart broke too—willingly, for our sake. On the Cross the incalculable weight of our sin broke His heart. He is forever the God of the broken-hearted. And He is forever a Redeemer; not only from sin, but of every tragedy and heartache and pain. If we will give our suffering to Him freely and expectantly, without fighting Him for "causing" it, we will find that He will make some form of creative use of it. He will not waste even pain and suffering.

A careful study of the Gospel accounts of Jesus' life on earth shows us that if we are willing to learn of Him, we will find His exact way of meeting our exact pain. For example, in Chapter 9 we considered the temptation Jesus experienced when He was invited to jump from the pinnacle of the Temple to prove that He was the Son of God. In this same temptation He has a definite word for those who are sufferers from accidents, too. There are many reasons why He didn't yield to this temptation, but one of them, I am sure, has to do with the questioning human heart which cries, "Why did God allow this terrible accident to happen?"

There is no pat answer here. But my heart rests on the fact that once more the Lord is saying to us, "Come now, and let us reason together."

Some years ago I spoke with a grandmother who had become bitter toward God because her grandchild had fallen to his death from her apartment window. "Why?" she wept. "Why would a God of love allow an innocent little boy to fall to his death?" In the first place, the boy's innocence had nothing to do with it. This woman had been faithful to her church, but this also had nothing to do with it.

Can we expect God to suspend the law of gravity because a Christian woman's grandchild leans too far out a sixth-story window? Our God is a God of order. But even above that, He remains a God of love. When I asked this grieving woman to consider that Jesus refused to

protect Himself by jumping from the Temple, she began
to see her way out of it. This did not bring her grandson
back, but it began to lessen her bitterness toward God.
If He had jumped from the pinnacle of the Temple in
order to prove His identity, this woman would have been
permanently and justifiably angry with God. She would
have remained grief-stricken. Grief alone is conquerable
in submission to Christ, but not if it is lashed to our hearts
by bands of resentment. After we prayed together this
woman said a penetrating thing: "Well, I guess the Lord
Jesus knew about my grandson the day He refused to
throw Himself from the pinnacle of the Temple." Then
her face brightened. "You know, I believe He would have
refused that temptation even if He had known that my
child would be the only one to die that way!"

I agree with her. And I remembered her words less
than two years ago as I stood by my beloved father's hospital bed. What does He have to say and what does He
do for those who lie, day after day, hour after tortured
hour, in hospitals and sickrooms? What does He have to
say and what does He do for those lying pinned under
wreckages of automobiles, or in the tangled cabins of
planes that have crashed? Even in our fine hospitals there
is suffering which no sedation can blot out or even dim.
What does God say and do here?

Do we dare approach one of these pain-tormented persons with the fact of Jesus Christ? If we know Him as
He is, yes. And we can be definite about it, too. In Mark
15:23 we are told that again Jesus Christ did not protect
His own humanity in His hour of most intense physical
pain. "And they offered him wine to drink, flavored with
myrrh; but He refused it."

Wine mixed with myrrh was a sedative in those days.
It was customary to offer it to the crucified to dull some
of their agony. It was offered to Jesus on His Cross. He
could have taken it and no one would have blamed Him.

But He was thinking of all of His loved ones who would not be able to find relief from their physical pain. He was, thinking of you. Of me. Of your loved ones. Of mine.

He was thinking, I now believe, of my own Father. During his last afternoon on earth, his suffering was intense. I was alone with him in his hospital room. Having learned that sometimes even the most sincere words are only rusty hooks jerked into the suffering of a human heart or body, I had just been standing there by his bed, holding his hand and saying nothing. He knew I was there. And he knew I was with him in it as much as I could be.

No matter how strong our faith in God, there are times when we don't dare bring it up as mere comfort. My Dad knew Christ intimately. He had already been showered with greeting cards, most of which reminded him that God would comfort him. Actually, he didn't even need to be reminded. His was a simple, strong, child-like faith. As I stood there and watched his suffering, I couldn't have attempted any kind of spiritual "chin-up." The words wouldn't have formed on my lips, least of all in my heart.

And so, I asked the Lord to show *me* something more about Himself in that dreadful moment. My own heart was breaking. But I didn't need to remind God of that. He already knew it. For several more minutes I just stood there beside the bed. And then I heard myself say quite quietly, "Dad, do you know what just came to me?"

He opened his eyes.

"I know now why Jesus refused to take the sedation they offered Him when He was hanging on the Cross. He knew this afternoon was coming up with us here and He didn't want you to think He'd take better care of Himself than can be taken of you!"

My Dad's mouth was too swollen from the leukemia blood blisters to smile. But since I was a child we had

had a special private signal for each other which meant, in a way only the two of us understood: "I get your point. I'm with you." We were a great deal alike and usually reacted the same way to a situation. And when we did, we passed this private signal—a big, exaggerated wink. In a moment, after I had reminded him that Jesus refused the sedative on the Cross, he turned his head toward me and winked. He knew it was true. And I sensed immediately that my Father had moved still closer to the Lord he loved.

All the way through the temptations in the wilderness, Jesus Christ had His mind on us and on our temptations.

All afternoon as He hung on the Cross, Jesus had His mind on us and on our sufferings.

His mind is still on us. And He has not forgotten what it is like to be one of us. There is a Man on the throne up there.

A Man-God who remembers well what it's like to be a human being. A God-Man who is still in it with us.

A Redeemer-God who does not encourage us to say, "life shouldn't be this way." But who urges us to accept life as it is; who still reminds us that "in this life you will have tribulation."

There is a Man-God on the throne up there who entered this life and took part in its suffering, so that He can face us now in the midst of our falling tears and continue to say, "Be of good cheer, I have overcome" all that can ever harm you permanently.

To anyone in any kind of suffering, Jesus Christ has earned the right to say, "Come unto me . . . bring your pain here to me. Together we will find a way to make use of it. I am your Redeemer. We will not waste a single tear."

# 12

# What Is His Death to Us Today?

# 12

---

## WHAT IS HIS DEATH TO US

## TODAY?

A Man named Jesus of Nazareth was crucified between two thieves on a Cross almost two thousand years ago.

Could this possibly have to do with us today? How do Christians dare to believe that this Man's death directly affects people walking in machine-made shoes on concrete sidewalks in this age of missiles and nylon?

John the Baptist said of Jesus of Nazareth, "Behold the Lamb of God which taketh away the sin of the world."

In the Book of Revelation, at the very end of the Bible, we are told that "the Lamb was slain before the foundation of the world." How is this related to the crucifixion of Jesus at Calvary less than two thousand years ago?

Is the Lamb spoken of by John the Baptist the same Lamb that was "slain before the foundation of the world"? If so, how do we manage to leap from before Creation to Calvary and arrive at today? And why do we hear so little about the "Lamb slain before the foundation of the world"? Is orthodox Christianity isolating the act of Calvary from this pre-world "Lamb slain"? Are we

limiting God to time? What indeed does the death of
Jesus Christ have to do with us today?

In Romans 5:10 we find some amazing words: "For if
as enemies we were reconciled to God through the death
of His Son, much more surely shall we, who have been
reconciled, be saved by His life."

In this chapter we are concerned with the first part of
this verse—our reconciliation through His death. How
are we reconciled through the death of Jesus of Nazareth
nearly two thousand years ago? Socrates died equally
nobly. No one has ever claimed to be "reconciled" by the
death of Socrates. Why? Because Socrates was not God
in the flesh. Jesus was. The death of Christ is valid to us
today *only* because of His identity.

Was that young Man, hanging on the Cross, God?

If He was, then the human heart is forced to look more
closely. The Bible tells us that "God was in Christ reconciling the world to Himself." If this is true, then God was
in that young Man hanging there in awful humiliation.

A disturbing question raises itself here. If this young
Man was God clothed in humanity, why did He cry out,
"Father, forgive them, for they know not what they do"?
Why did He scream in His darkest moment, "My God,
My God, why hast thou forsaken me?" If Jesus was God
visiting this earth, to whom was He praying on the Cross?
Was He praying to Himself?

Here we must remember that Jesus of Nazareth was all
that could be contained of God in a human being. There
is far too much of God to be fully held by one Man.
When He visited this earth, He came as one of us. A
human being. "He had to be made like His brothers in
every respect." As Jesus hung on the Cross, He was all
that could be contained of God in a human body, but He
was also utterly human. And as a Son He was in all things
submissive to His Father. On the Cross, Jesus the Man
was praying to the Father-God. He was at once God and

Man. The Son of God and the Son of Man. The Man-God. The God-Man. To our mortal minds, mystery perhaps graciously obscures *how* this was possible. But God's method is not the point where we are concerned. Our part is to realize, once and for all, that throughout eternity no one will ever discover one tiny contradiction between the Father and the Son. Their heart is one. Their intent is one. Jesus went the whole way and declared, "I and my Father *are* one."

God was in Christ, then, on the Cross, reconciling the world unto Himself. The entire key to the Christian faith is our awareness of the true identity of the One who hung there that dark day on Calvary. If Jesus was merely another great teacher, His death can have no more to do with me now than the death of Socrates, another great teacher. I can be inspired by it, but how can I be reconciled to God by it? My admiration of "Socrates drinking the hemlock and Jesus on the rood" can inspire me, but I can also be depressed by their noble spirits. I can be made to feel guilty, knowing that I could not meet death in the same exalted way in which they met it.

But if Jesus of Nazareth was God Himself visiting the earth, then His death on the Cross automatically involves me, since I, as a created being, have a primal relationship with my Creator. Sin in me has jerked me loose from the original harmonious oneness with God, but there lingers in every person the need to return. To be reconciled.

Even if we don't yet see *how* this reconciliation takes place, there is at least hope for it, *if* the Young Man on the Cross is one with God.

In my own mind there was for some time deep confusion about the actual connection between the death of Christ and humanity. I read that "there is no remission of sin, except by the shedding of blood." I believed this. I still do. I read and spoke and wrote of the "finished work of Calvary." That I was deeply involved in it, I had no doubt. That it affected me directly, I had no doubt. The Atonement of Christ had somehow made me *at one* with God. I knew it intellectually and I knew it experientially.

But I also retained some kind of inner dullness and confusion over the explanation that Jesus "took my sins away" that one dark day on the hill outside the gates of Jerusalem.

I did not doubt it. I knew that since my life was linked with His, since I had recognized Him as my Saviour, peace had come to me. And with it a new vital interest in all of life and a hope that could not have been conjured up by my nimble imagination. But, over and over again, I saw the same confusion and dullness, the same lack of comprehension in the eyes of other persons to whom I was trying to explain His death. It wasn't the stubborn resistance of a human being fighting God. It was genuine confusion as to how His death so long ago could possibly affect us now.

I became painfully aware of the need to allow the Cross of Christ to emerge from its Jewish matrix and let it touch the hearts of today's pagans. After all, Jesus made it clear that God would no longer limit His pursuit to one people.

"I, if I be lifted up from the ground [on the Cross] will draw *all* men unto me."

"Come unto me, *all* ye that labor and are heavy laden. . . ."

In this chapter I am not attempting to set forth a doctrine of the atonement as such. And to those of you who hold no confusion concerning the death of Christ, I ask that you realize I am attempting to express some of the insight which liberated me from my confusion and lack of understanding. Primarily, I am trying to communicate here with those who have not had a doctrinal background. Those who, like myself ten years ago, are either in the dark where the Cross is involved, or who find their hearts locked against a theory concerning it.

Instead of an explanation of the Atonement, which has already been done in more scholarly fashion than I could manage, I want to speak of *the One* who made the Atonement possible. I have found Him to be the drawing power, just as He said He would be. I will not speak so much of what He did on the Cross, as of Who it was Who did it. This approach not only melted my heart and quieted my confusion, it has melted the hearts and quieted the confusion in almost every other person with whom I have shared it.

I do not believe there is any new viewpoint concerning the Cross of Christ. "The Lamb was slain before the foundation of the world." Our part is only to stay open to an ever deepening understanding of it. My own heart rebels at a pat explanation of His Cross. To me it is the open door to a living relationship, not a procedure which can be contained in words. We dare not shut up the Christ of the Cross in a box! Even if we try, He will break out of it, because He is alive and because He is too big for our boxes.

No one knows more clearly than I, who tried too long to make the grade by my intellect, that these things cannot be known intellectually. They must be revealed to us by the Spirit of God. To the natural man they are foolish. And yet, I now believe that God will move heaven and earth to reveal Himself clearly to any open heart. He demands far less conformity in our thinking than the average Christian demands. He respects the unfathomable depths of the human personality all the way. He knew "He had to be made like His brothers in every respect." He does not ask us to accept some worded explanation of His Cross. If He did, He would have settled for the Biblical statement that "the Lamb was slain before the foundation of the world." He 'did a much more patient and gracious thing. A much clearer thing. He came to earth and allowed Himself to be slain before our eyes! He asks that we accept *Him*.

Jesus always makes issues clear. We have already said that His one motive for coming to earth was to clarify, once and for all, the true nature of the Father. I said this from a platform once and a dear lady approached me afterward with this admonition: "Genie, you must never say again that Jesus came to show us what the Father's heart is like." When I asked why, she simply said, "It isn't correct doctrine. He came to die!"

I quite agree. But His death is the supreme showing of the Father's heart. It is the identity of the One on the Cross that reconciles me. It is the identity of the One on the Cross that causes me even to see that I need to be reconciled.

It is not the death alone, it is the One involved in the death. It is His very attitude as He hung there that affects me so directly. I am struck by His willingness to go through with the only means He knew could ever melt the human heart into a desire to be reconciled to Himself. He "personally carried our sins onto the cross." And with them He experienced the agony of their consequences.

Over and over I am asked, "Why did Jesus have to go to the Cross? Couldn't God have done it another way?" I am convinced that He could not. If He could have, He would have. Love shows itself supremely when it is laying itself at the feet of the rebellious loved one. Love shows itself supremely when it exposes its goodness without defense to the fury of the rebellious loved one. As I see the pure goodness of God on the Cross, the guilt of the hammer blows becomes mine. The conniving mind of the Sanhedrin arouses guilt in me. I am painfully affected by the goodness which drove self-centered humanity to try to do away with Him.

Recently a young person asked a provocative question: "If there was no other way to be rid of our sins, why are we supposed to be so sorry Jesus died on the Cross?" We are not to feel sorry. We are to rejoice! There was no other way, and I can never accept the notion that Christ opened His arms on the Cross and experienced death to make us feel sorry. He did it because He knew there was no other way to let us see the gaping chasm between Himself and His loved ones—who had jerked themselves out of His loving will by their self-willed determination to be their own masters.

Desperately, we need to begin to look at ourselves and at God as living persons in relationship with one another. Desperately we need to put aside for one clear moment any preconceived theories about some magical theological performance on Calvary and look clearly at ourselves and at God.

He is not foisting explanations on us, He is still offering Himself to us. Our part is to take stock of our relationship with Him. Either we belong to Him, or we still belong to ourselves. Either we have returned to God's original plan for us, or we haven't. In the beginning God created us to belong to Himself. We have wrenched free of Him. And yet no one has ever been able to wrench free of His love. He proved this when He came to earth Himself and showed us His heart on the Cross. In Jesus Christ, the Father made a way for us to come back. No one can explain forgiveness, but anyone can experience it. And only those who have experienced the unexplainable forgiveness of God, through response to Jesus Christ, are the peaceful ones.

Human nature is not at home orbiting independently in its own sphere. It was created to be linked with God, and although it had the power to jerk itself away from

Him, it does not have the power, nor the desire, to come back. Anyone who longs for peace with God has gotten that longing directly from God through His Holy Spirit. Anyone who has returned to the love relationship with Him, which He intended in the first place, has been brought back into it through response to the wooing of Jesus Christ.

This need in the human personality for forgiveness, for reconciliation with God, is not limited to religious theory. Dr. Alphonse Maeder, a noted Swiss psychiatrist, has written a clear explanation of what he feels happens in the human personality that causes the whole pattern of life to be distorted—to become unharmonized, self-centered. In his book, *Ways to Psychic Health*, Dr. Maeder writes: "Sin, evil, committing the forbidden deed constitute a violation of the divine command, a rebellion of the self against God. Herewith the creature repudiates its dependence upon the creator in order to be its own master. As a result the order of creation is pierced, the breach is opened between the creature and its creator, and the human being possesses only a relative, limited independence. When he elevates himself arbitrarily to an absolute, independent being—something central in him is broken, namely, the inner bond with his origin and His Divine Master. He transforms himself into a titanic but also an uprooted being. The original love for and trust in God transform themselves into an unchained, demonic and destructive egoism as demonstrated by world history up to the present time." [1]

The Bible declares that we have "all sinned and come short of the glory of God." To the modern mind Dr. Maeder's description goes straight to the mark. This universal state of falling short of what God has a right to expect of us (had not the sin of self-assertion twisted us out of shape), shows itself in various stages of personality defects, but it always shows itself. There *is*, there can be, no integration, no harmony of the human personality which is still cut off from God. We do become "titanic," and we are all "uprooted beings." We can accurately paraphrase the Biblical estimate of human nature by saying, "All have become titanic, (enormously self-willed) because all are uprooted beings—having cut themselves off from God."

Further on in his book Dr. Maeder writes, "Then like a ray of light in the darkness I was struck by the words: 'For the Son of Man is come to seek and to save that which was lost' [Sinful, uprooted, grown enormous in its own estimate]. It appeared to me as the perfect model for our psychotherapeutic activity. These words have never lost their effect upon me and have repeatedly strengthened me in moments of despair." [2]

No one needs to stay "uprooted" and unreconciled. But God knew that the alienation from Himself by sin in the human heart was so great that He would somehow have to produce the desire in us for reconciliation before He could offer it.

And so He came to earth in Jesus of Nazareth, the one sinless Man who ever lived on our planet. His very presence caused His death. The presence of the God-Man in the midst of the selfish corruption of the religious and political little men of His earthly day, forced them to try to annihilate Him! When Jesus walked the earth men did one of two things. They either gave themselves to Him or they tried to do away with Him. His goodness shows our sin so painfully that the human self must take some action. Religion and pious beliefs do not affect people this way. Only when the human heart sees God as He is in Jesus Christ does this violent reaction take place. As I realized I stood in the Presence of such goodness, the very goodness of God Himself, I was driven to try to blot Him out or to run to Him. His pure and holy Person in our midst, once we recognize Him as being God Himself, forces us either to commit ourselves to Him or try to blot Him out by disbelief.

As I saw the God-Man hanging on His Cross asking forgiveness for me, I was stunned by the sharp cracking of my own defenses. As I saw Him, I saw myself and the contrast was so pain-filled I longed to be blinded by it! Blindness would have been a temporary relief. At least I wouldn't have had to look at myself any longer. Did Paul, as Saul of Tarsus, experience this? He told it well: "Due to the brilliancy of that intense light, I was blinded."

The God-Man hanging on His Cross, with His arms stretched out toward the whole world, looked at me and I knew I could never bear not to look back at Him for all eternity. But there was the vast dark discord between us. Suddenly I wanted to press my ears shut against the most hideous sound I had ever heard! But pressing my hands to my ears did no good. This was not something I heard with my ears. It was an inner distortion, a discord screeching at the very center of my being. I became aware for the first time that I lived out of harmony with God and all of His universe. I failed to shut it out by much talking and it clanged the louder when I tried to shout my denial that Jesus Christ was God! There was in me no way to contain the dreadful disharmony of my life alongside His, once I had seen Him. "If I am like this and if He is like that, I can no longer live with myself as I am. No human being could experience such discord and live!"

This was something of my own experience long before I knew God had said, "No human being can see Me and live." To me this does not mean I will be struck dead physically if I see God. It means that seeing Him as He was in Christ on the Cross brought me to such an awareness of the discord in my own life that I could no longer bear it.

This would be called by some, "conviction of sin." It is. Still I am helpless against sin. I cannot live with it, but I cannot rid myself of it. The more I try, the louder grows the screaming discord around me.

But the noise has stopped now. I have linked my life with His. I knew that I had seen God on His Cross, and from the seeing came the equivalent of death to the screaming disharmony within me, but new life to me!

The dictionary definition of "reconciliation" is "to harmonize." Looking at the God-Man dying on His Cross brought me to my knees, not in adoration at first, but in sheer weakness against the pounding thunder of the discord rolling around me. Obviously, it had been there before. I only became aware of it when I believed that I stood in the Presence of the Saviour-God who created me. Of the Man-God who died on a cross for love of me. In my blessed desperation, I cried out for forgiveness. I think I really meant to cry for peace and an end to that discord! But the word forgiveness forced itself up from my broken heart.

And then there was peace.

I see now that Jesus, the Son, was not "paying an angry Father" for my sins. The Father was paying with His own God-heart on the Cross, as a mother pays when she goes on loving a disobedient, ungrateful child. I see now that the Father is not merely "accepting me, loathesome creature that I am," because His Son did what He did. I see now that the Father and the Son are in this together. They are one. The heart I saw breaking on Calvary was the very heart of God Himself.

Because I have at last seen the intention toward me of the heart of God, I am harmonized. And I am being harmonized. Jarring discords come and go outwardly. I rebel. I weep. Too often I am unloving and impatient. But as the discords come, they go, because deep within my essential self is harmony with God through what I have at last seen Him to be in the death of Jesus on the Cross.

We are reconciled through His death, *not* by some magical theological performance. After all, the "Lamb *was* slain before the foundation of the world." Jesus broke into human history to prove this! On Calvary, Christ was merely laying bare the heart of God as it has always been. The Father's heart was not changed as Jesus hung on the Cross. It was revealed.

I wouldn't have known I needed harmonizing if I hadn't been permitted to see the heart of God *exposed* at last on the Cross. I wouldn't have dared look at myself. If that had not been God Himself on His Cross, there would have been no hope for me.

No human being on earth needs to stay out of harmony with God. God has revealed Himself in Jesus and no one needs ever again to worry and wonder about Him. The great simplification has taken place. "The Son of Man has come to save that which was lost [cut off]."

Another question can be raised here. *How* am I reconciled? Jesus said, "If you have seen Me, you have seen the Father." Quite simply, I believe I was reconciled with God by *looking* at the One who died on the Cross. But it is not my looking that does this, it is what I see when I look. I see at last something of what God is really like. The veil of the Temple was torn from the top to the bottom when Jesus died. So was the heart of God. It is open now. Anyone can look inside and discover for himself what everyone longs to know—the authentic intention of God toward the entire human race.

We are reconciled by exposure to the true nature of God as we see it in Jesus Christ on His Cross. In Him is our way back. In Him "who committed no sin, neither was deceit found in His mouth; who did not return the insult when He was insulted; who did not threaten when abused—who personally in His own body carried our sins onto the Cross, so that [seeing Him as He is] we might abandon our sins and live for righteousness."

His heart has already been exposed to us. There remains only the exposure of our hearts to Him.

# 13

# What Is His Life to Us Today?

# 13

---

## WHAT IS HIS LIFE TO US
## TODAY?

When Jesus personally in His own body "carried our sins
onto the cross," He was identifying with us in the ultimate degree.

No one can understand how He "carried our sins." His
ways are higher than our ways. But as I realize that He
did carry my sins onto His Cross, if I am thinking at all,
I must also realize that He experienced their painful and
frustrating consequences, too. Sin cannot be contained
within the human heart without sin's accompanying consequences. When I am rebellious, my whole emotional
and nervous system suffers. My body suffers. As I continue
to rebel, the suffering increases. A resentment held in my
own heart toward someone else causes me more pain and
poison than it causes the one whom I resent. Medical
science backs this up one hundred per cent. Medical
statistics show that at least eighty per cent of all physical
illness is emotional or mental in origin.

Think, then, of the magnified suffering of Christ as He
carried the sins of every human being onto His Cross! No
wonder He died. The darkness of that accumulated sin

caused His humanity to cry out, "My God, My God, why hast thou forsaken me?" The weight of that sin broke His heart. He was sinless in Himself, but the terrible consequence of sin in our lives is no mystery to God. He experienced it all on the Cross.

To me, this has directly to do with my own willingness to allow Him to live His resurrection life in me now. Over and over we hear people say, "I know what Jesus Christ would do in my circumstances, but He was God's Son. He had the power to do it. I'm just a human being."

As far as it goes, this is true. But if a human being has linked his life with the life of the One who got up and left His tomb, that human being has access to His very life today!

As He has identified with us, so we can identify with Him. Peaceful Christians live the exchanged life. The Apostle Paul wrote, "I am crucified with Christ; nevertheless I live, yet not I, but *Christ liveth in me.*"

And the Christ who lives in the human life of His followers knows how it feels to bear the consequences of sin. Too many new followers expect to get off the hook entirely where the error of their old lives is concerned. I know a woman whose shattered life is still shattered, even after she has turned to Christ, because she blocks Him at every turn. Her husband is dead, and since she drank heavily for twelve years before turning to Christ, the courts have put her two small children in the care of her mother. She has been a believer only about nine months, and although I neither question her sincerity (as far as she sees) nor the willingness of God to cooperate in her tragedy, she is standing still because she will not let go her demand that God should fix everything up at once. "I've turned to Christ now, why should I go on suffering? Why can't I have my children back now?"

She cannot seem to grasp the fact that He is involved in this predicament right now with her. When anyone links his life with Christ, He in turn links His with that human life. But He works realistically, as things are. This woman is not ready to care for her children yet. Even if she were, the courts would not release them to her. If she could see that in her every troubled day she has the choice of allowing Him to be Himself in her, she would be enabled by His life in her to make her way back to normalcy.

The Bible clearly states, "As ye sow, so shall ye reap." There is no promise anywhere that any human being will be exempt from the consequences of his sin, past or present. He can be empowered not to sin in the same way again, but God does not make pets of His followers. If we break ourselves over His moral laws, we must be willing to submit to the consequences. And we can do this if we know that we do have access to His life every minute of our lives.

The Father did not make an exception for His sinless Son, and He would be unkind in the final analysis if He made exceptions for us. Jesus experienced the consequences of human sin on His Cross. He knows what it is like. He is not asking that we do anything which He Himself has not already done.

As I read through the daily newspapers, I am constantly amazed at how people who probably do not know of the tremendous potential of the human life linked with the life of Christ, can go through the torment of the daily tragedies.

I have tried life both ways. For thirty-three years of my life, I lived it alone, orbiting independently of God. For ten years I have known the stability and security of my life linked with His life. I have known the certainty of His life within me. Actually, during the ten years as His follower, I have had more problems and more hardships and more grief than in all the thirty-three years before. And yet, the pressure has been off! I have not been alone

in them. No matter what happens, if I am willing to remember and act on the fact that He is living His life
within mine, I find unlimited resources for anything that
happens.

Occasionally, I must still cope with a consequence of
my life before Christ invaded it. By now, I almost welcome these consequences. They're far from comfortable,
but when I allow Him to be Himself in me as they occur,
I find I emerge stronger, even more peaceful and with a
sharpened sense of humor and wisdom.

By now, you know that the theme of this book is the
necessity for us to find out what God is really like. I return to that theme here. If your concept of God is distorted or superficial or false, it will be of little help to
you to know that He lives in you. But if you know Him
as He is knowable through a continuing discovery of Jesus
Christ, you will find your rebellions dwindling. Few persons openly doubt the power of God. But most of us act
as though we do doubt His intentions toward us!

He is not a separate, remote stranger living within you.
He is your Creator. And because He created you, He
knows your inner, true self better than you will ever know
it. We do not need to master a set of victorious life techniques, as I once believed. We need to discover the true
nature of the Master! Once we discover Him as He is, we
begin to feel at home with Him. We begin to wonder why
we ever struggled to win our own victories. We relax at
the center of our personalities. We enter into the rest He
promised, if we come to Him and learn of Him.

This is not an easily grasped truth. God does not whisk
us on a celestial carpet from the realm of stumbling,
struggling, defeated Christians to the smooth and rutless
realm of perfect sainthood. It is a daily life together. Our
lives and His life. And its route is mountainous and sometimes very slow and rough. There are detours and road
work along the way. There are also four-laned highways

here and there, but even on the four-laned highways there is the danger that we begin to feel too confident and exceed the speed limits. Still, all along the way, realistic and rough as it is, there are our lives together with His. Every bump we take, He takes, too.

A long, hard trip is never so tiring or discouraging if we have good company on the way. I traveled alone on my speaking engagements for almost eight years. Now I have a partner who travels with me. We can be together twenty-four hours a day and never tire of each other's company. A speaking tour of twice the length tires me far less now than when I traveled alone.

If this can be true with two human beings, what endless resources are available when we realize that He is not only with us, but in us, wherever the road goes.

In the preceding chapter we looked at the first part of Romans 5:10. It might be well to examine the whole verse again, with emphasis on the last part in this chapter. "For if as enemies we were reconciled to God through the death of His Son, much more surely shall we, who have been reconciled, be saved by His life."

"... *much more surely shall we, who have been reconciled, be saved by His life.*"

Is there a general confusion of terms here among Christians? According to Paul, we are *saved* by His *life*. What does this mean? Surely no one will argue the fact that we need to be saved daily. I am not speaking of the new birth here. We will go into that in another chapter. Perhaps we have oversimplified and limited the word *saved*. Personally, I agree with the obvious implication of Paul here. I am *being saved* by His life. This is undoubtedly a continuous thing which is taking place with me, because His life is continuous. I need to be saved minute by minute from my own willful nature. And this is made possible by the life of Christ in me. In each instance I choose whether I will be myself in a certain circumstance, or

whether I will let Him be Himself. He has the power to
take me past the rough places. He has the power to lift
me over the mudholes. He has the power to straighten me
out when I try to take the curves too fast.

And this power is not some sudden magical influx which
comes bolting down to me out of the blue. It is Christ
Himself with me and in me.

The power to live sane, creative, mature lives is not
a separate gift from God. It is in the very Person of Christ
Himself. Power does not come in a package. We cannot
store it up. It is not a static commodity in any sense. It
is as ever present as Christ.

I once heard the Trinity explained this way: God the
Father is *God for us.* His intentions are all toward us. God
the Son is *God with us,* and in Him is the same nature as
in the Father. The same intentions. The Holy Spirit is
*God in us,* enabling us to respond to Himself. The Holy
Spirit, of course, has the same nature as the Father and
the Son.

Our response to God, as we can know Him in the three
persons of the Godhead, is conditioned by our recognition
of the constant, indwelling Presence of the Spirit. When
Jesus was on earth He spoke and lived and communicated
His love directly with those He met. The same thing is
happening now in the Presence of the Holy Spirit of this
same Christ within.

No one can ever fully understand or express the Trinity.
But as far as I can see, the only thing we need to know
for certain is that although they are expressed as three
Persons, there is absolutely no contradiction among them.
They are one. The Son, Jesus Christ, returned to His
Father. We'll see Him one day and I'm sure He will still
be in a body we can recognize. But He is with us and in
us just as surely now in the Person of His Holy Spirit.

It is really a foolish prayer to ask God for power!

All power to live safe, sane, creative lives on this earth

is available in the Person of the Spirit of Christ with us and in us. We draw power from His Person, therefore it is ridiculous to ask God for what we already have been given when He gave us His Spirit.

However new you are in your Christian life, the moment you opened your life to Christ His Spirit invaded your body, your personality, your mind, your emotions. No one but God understands how this comes about. He does, however, so I find I don't need to waste my energies worrying about it. If you have received Christ, He is there. Your part now is to learn of Him. Learn how to live in harmony with Him. This, of course, is called obedience. After all, He is your Master now. Once you were your own. No more.

If you have not yet opened your life to all you know of God in Jesus Christ, you have this up ahead. When you do, He will come. "Behold, I stand at the door and knock; if any man will open the door, I will come in and sup with him and he with Me."

From that moment on, He will be in you and with you, even when you eat! These words, "I will come in and sup with him and he with Me," are from the Book of Revelation in the Bible. Words spoken by the risen and ascended Christ. He has not changed just because He has returned to His glory. He is still the same gentle, careful, patient, considerate Lord. Just because He has returned to His glory apparently gives Him no license to beat down your door.

"Behold, I stand at the door and knock. . . ."

He waits for you to decide. But when you open the door He will come in. And speaking as the resurrected and glorified Christ, He took time to remind us that when He comes in, He will sup with us and we with Him. Jesus Christ is no less mindful of our human need to know He will be with us, caring about us even in the small daily things now, than He was when He walked this earth.

experiencing the same human needs. We need constantly to remember, "There *is* a Man on the throne up there!"

When things are going rather well for us, we find it quite possible to believe that Christ lives in us. That we are saved from ourselves by His life. When things go wrong, it is not so easy to believe it. Some spoiled-brat streak in all of us seems to cling to the idea that if God is really near by, things should be going well for us!

Here again is the tremendous necessity for us to know what He is like. He reminds us, "In the world you are under pressure. . . ." Nowhere in the Bible does God promise to make life easy for anyone. But He does promise to be with us in all things. And if we have learned and are continuing to learn what He is really like, we find our trouble spots, not obnoxious things to jump over or avoid, but opportunities to face up to the unrealities within us, opportunities to try out His life in us, opportunities to enter into a still closer and more dynamic relationship with Him.

Everything may seem to be going wrong in your life now, but all power to see you through your present trouble is in His Person, and He has said, "Lo, I am with you always." He is there, and when He is there all the power you need is available for you to use.

The power-filled Christian life is merely a life in contact with Jesus Christ. And "neither death nor life, neither angels nor mighty ones, neither present nor future affairs, neither powers of the heights nor of the depths, neither anything else created shall be able to separate us from the love of God that is in Christ Jesus our Lord."

# 14

## What Is the New Birth?

# 14

---

## WHAT IS THE NEW BIRTH?

I am now convinced that although the new birth and conversion can take place simultaneously, this is not always the case. In fact, years may separate the two.

I happen to be one of those persons who is reasonably sure of the time of my *conversion* to Christ. On October 2, 1949, I consciously placed the controls of my life in His hands by faith in my scant but sure knowledge of who He was.

Concerning the actual time of my *new birth*, I am not so certain. I was brought up in a Christian church and as a child my mother taught me to pray. But in my teens I rebelled against all I had seen of religion and declared my independence from anyone's concept of God.

My new birth could have taken place about six weeks before my conversion, which occurred in a hotel room in New York City, in the presence of Christ and the dear friend who had made Him real to me. She and I had our first conversation about Christ and His claims on our lives six weeks earlier. While I was far from willing then to rest my case in His hands, I know that during those next six weeks another dimension seemed added to my life. I faced things in myself which I had never dared face be-

129

fore. Many of the things I had loved seemed suddenly empty. I was both restless and hopeful, disturbed and interested.

In retrospect, I can see that, whether I realized it or not then, I seemed not to be alone during those weeks immediately before my conversion. I was disagreeing with my friend. At times I experienced real fear, but all around me was a Kindness which I could not explain. And in me there was an energy and an interest in life which I had long ago traded for what I hoped was a sophisticated, if unavoidable, boredom.

Did my *new birth* take place at the beginning of our talks six weeks before my *conversion?* Did it take place, as some would believe, when I was a child, exposed to the Christian faith by my mother and my Sunday school teachers? Certainly there was no outward evidence of it until my conversion at thirty-three. But to me, the actual time of my *new birth* is not only unknowable to me, it is irrelevant.

Jesus told the intellectual and highly educated Nicodemus, "You need to be born (again) from above." He also said, "Unless a person is born from above he cannot see the kingdom of God." That we must all undergo the new birth is a fact, if we believe that Jesus Christ spoke with the authority of God. But many are confused right here, because if they cannot remember or point to an exact time of their new birth, they doubt that it ever took place.

As always, Jesus tried to make this clear, too. If we are confused on it, it is due to careless teaching or careless reading of what He said. While He made it plain that we must be born again, He also made it equally plain that it is not something that we do. To this same Nicodemus who asked, "How can a man be born when he is old?" Jesus explained, "What is born of the flesh is flesh; and what is born of the Spirit is spirit . . . The wind blows where it pleases and though you hear the sound of it, you neither know whence it comes or whither it goes. *It is the same with everyone who is born of the Spirit.*"

Could He have said it more clearly? When we are born the first time, from our mother's womb, we are born into the wide but limited wonder of the physical universe. But when we are born the second time from above, we are *by God's Spirit* born into the even wider and eternal wonder of the Kingdom of God. When and how it happens is God's doing.

In his book, *Christian Life and the Unconscious*, Dr. Ernest White has helped greatly to clear away my confusion about the nature of the new birth and conversion. Here is some of Dr. White's excellent explanation showing that the two need not be confused.

"I wish to distinguish between new birth and conversion. . . . The word conversion means a turning, a change of direction, an alteration in mental attitude and belief. It does not necessarily imply new birth. For instance, a Protestant may be converted to Roman Catholicism, or vice versa, either subsequently to or before his new birth. A Buddhist might become a Mohammedan, but this would not entail new birth in the Christian sense of the word. Conversion is usually an act of the will, and is often accompanied by some degree of emotional disturbance. . . . St. James writes in his epistle, 'If any of you do err from the truth, and one convert him, let him know, that he which converteth the sinner from the error of his way shall save a soul from death.'

"In this example we see the possibility of one man converting another. Only the Spirit of God can create new life. Conversion, then, is a conscious act of the will by which a man turns to God, or turns from one opinion or course of conduct to another. It is a conscious and deliberate movement of the mind in a new direction, but it is not the same thing as the new birth." [1]

I was *converted* (made to see and to agree to change the course of my life) by my friend, Ellen Riley Urquhart, and I made that decision to begin the new direction of my life on October 2, 1949. She converted me, but she could not *create in me a new life*. Only the Spirit of God could do this. Just when He did this is not important.

Dr. White holds the belief that, unlike *conversion*, the *new birth* is an unconscious process, apart from the will of man, worked out in the spiritual depths of the human personality by the Spirit of God. Sometimes the effects of this entrance into the depths of the human personality, or the unconscious, by the Spirit shows up immediately in our conscious behavior. In others the realization of the new birth is a slow and gradual process. In some it bursts upon the conscious mind like a sunrise. Then again, in a personality of a different temperament, it comes slowly like spring over the frozen ground.

As I understand it, my new birth occurred when Christ Himself invaded my personality. Mine is a fairly sudden temperament, and when I made my decision to change my course and follow Him as my Saviour and Master, the signs that I *had* been born again showed up rather quickly. I think, mainly, because in that sense I had "become as a little child." I was looking for signs of my new life! I was excited and expectant. I am not timid by nature. If I see something or believe something, I am ready immediately to dive into it all the way. It would be an even more perplexing world than it is if we were all like me. And so the error in doubting your own new birth, just because the effects of it don't show up at once emblazoned upon the night sky of your personality, is a great error indeed.

In my book *Woman to Woman*, I shared one or two letters from persons who doubted their new birth because they didn't *feel* "born again." My mail continues to be spattered with these sad pleas and complaints about God.

Two things and two things only are important where the new birth is concerned. First, Jesus says we must be born again. Second, if we have come to see Him at all clearly, we know that He is eager to bring this birth about. When He said, "The wind blows where it pleases," I don't think He meant that He was willing to come more quickly to some. I think He was merely trying to clarify the facts about the new birth for us. We cannot always know the exact time the Spirit comes to make His home in the depths of our beings. *But we can know that He is always willing and eager to come.*

"If any man will open the door, I will come in." Again Jesus made it as plain as possible. But even if He hadn't put it in so many words, is there anything in the attitude of Christ on His Cross which would cause you to believe that He was not eager for you to experience the benefits of His agony there? Weren't His arms stretched out toward the whole world? Is there anything in the Personality of Jesus Christ which would cause you to think He is not dependable? If He said so definitely that we must be born again, do you think He would fail to keep His part of the transaction? If He bothered to remind us that it was a spiritual birth, made possible only by the Spirit of God, do you think He would fail in doing for you what He knows *only He could do for you?*

It is all important that we remember that the three Persons of the Trinity are One. They do not in any way contradict or disagree with one another. One does not act conversely to the deep longing of the other. If the Father sent His Only-begotten Son to reach us and bring us back to Himself, would the Son or the Spirit oppose Him in it? They are One. They think as One, they long as One, they act as One.

If your ears are open to hear the Son of God tell you that you are in need of the new birth, immediately you will find the Spirit pressing against your heart for entrance!

The new birth is supernatural. It is the entrance into you of the Spirit of God Himself. It occurs in one moment of time. But since it apparently occurs in your unconscious depths, you are not always immediately aware of a cataclysmic invasion.

More than this, it is realized by faith. And if this sounds nebulous to you, think of it this way. Remember that *your faith is in direct proportion to your knowledge of the true character of God.* You won't have to whip it up and think positive thoughts in order to convince yourself that the Spirit of God has invaded your mortal life. You will only need to remember that God is discoverable to anyone. We can all know Him and His intentions toward us when we know Jesus Christ. We have no quixotic unknown quantity to reckon with here. We have an open fact. God has exposed His heart on the Cross in His Son. Jesus on the Cross is what God thinks of you. Jesus on the Cross is the extent of His love. Jesus on the Cross is the extent of His eagerness to be one with you.

In speaking of the supernatural character of the new birth, Dr. White writes: "When I say that it is supernatural I mean that it occurs outside the natural laws which govern the material universe, and it cannot be brought about by any effort of man. The new birth is the implantation of divine life, or eternal life, in the spirit of man. It cannot be achieved or attained, for it is the gift of God." [2]

Dr. Henry Drummond once wrote that a man can no more make himself a member of the Kingdom of God than a member of the vegetable kingdom can lift itself into the animal kingdom.

We can no more know the exact time of the implanting of the seed of eternal life in the human heart than we can know the exact moment when the male cell uniting with the female cell brings a new life into being. In fact, it is only by a discovery of modern science that we even know of this uniting of the male and female human cells.

Some new Christians are peaceful and joyous at once. Others find assurance coming more slowly. Neither case is necessarily normal. *The basis of the Christian life is Jesus Christ Himself.* If we could only see this quickly, we would go on depending upon Him because of what we know of Him, and refuse to be upset by what we feel concerning our own spiritual state.

I cannot resist mentioning here, once more, the danger in trying to pour new Christians into a mold of artificial piety. Jesus Christ invades the human heart because the impetus is from His side. And He always works with what He finds there according to what He knows both of Himself and of the person whose life He has invaded. God never works from the outside. If you are a new Christian, don't try to imitate the Christians you admire. Don't try to speak as they speak. Be yourself in Christ. You cannot trust yourself, but you can trust the One who has come to live in your personality. And you can depend upon it, at all times and under all circumstances, that He is working by His Spirit in the depths of your personality. He never sleeps, but He works while you sleep. Sometimes He can do more if you are asleep! Then your conscious mind is not trying to be something or someone you are not. He is interested always in the essential you—as He alone knows you to be.

If we cannot know the time of the new birth, then how are we to be sure it has occurred?

First of all, we can take Christ's word for it. "If any man will open the door, I will come in. . . ."

But aside from this, there are a few new signs which show up in us, too. First of all, there is a natural, almost unexplainable, desire to be with other Christians. This too may come gradually. It may seem to be absent at first.

But wait. Don't jump at conclusions about the absence of God's life in your life merely because you happen to be shy or antisocial. Be realistic about your own personality as well as His. The second indication which usually appears is a desire to pray. Most likely not in the unfortunate, unnatural "praying voice" of some other Christians you know, but it will become just as natural for you to cry out to God, even wordlessly, as it is for a newborn baby to cry for attention from its mother. And one other indication of the new birth within you (and this one may come first of all) is that you will want to bring others into the same new life with Christ.

Many sincere Christians believe that the proof of the new birth always shows itself in a desire to read the Bible. I know this is frequently true. However, I have found it not always the case. Many times the new Christian is slow about becoming interested in the Bible simply because he happens to have only a King James Version. I have nothing against the King James Version, but it is difficult to understand for those who have not yet been exposed to Bible teaching. If you are a new Christian, try one of the new versions. In this book, I am using the King James, along with the *Berkeley Version* of the Bible. I particularly recommend the Berkeley translation because the music of the King James Version is rather well preserved in it, but also because I feel the footnotes are unique. They will help you understand how to live your Christian life. They will not be over your head theologically and scholastically, as are many of the other Bibles with marginal notes. Along with the *Berkeley Version*, I also use *The Amplified New Testament* which gives all the possible meanings of the Greek. And no new Christian should be without the Phillips translation of the New Testament, which is certainly worded for the contemporary reader with little or no Bible training.

We are also told in the Bible that when the Spirit lives

within us, He will witness to His own Presence there. This is true. However, too often the new convert who has met Christ as an adult is still so keenly aware of his own nature that this alone is not enough to give assurance to some overly sensitive souls. Particularly to those who have not yet come to the place of believing something to be true because the Bible says it is. Do not misunderstand me here. The Bible declares that the Spirit will witness to His own Presence simply because it is true. He does. But some highly neurotic, oversensitive persons cannot at first quiet themselves enough to grasp this inner witness.

Most important to remember, where the new birth is concerned, is that if you have come to believe that Jesus Christ is who He claimed to be—one with the Father—and if you have placed your faith in Him, *He has come to indwell your life.* We lay hold of this fact by faith. Not faith in the fact, but faith in the Person who said He would come.

# 15

## What Is Conversion?

# 15

---

## WHAT IS CONVERSION?

What I share in this and the preceding chapter on the new birth and conversion is not intended to stir up and confuse, but to clarify. If there is no confusion on your part about these matters, I submit that there is an enormous amount of it among many persons.

For example, I find that I am far from alone in my frequent puzzling about certain older Christians who seem not to have taken seriously Jesus' commandment that we love one another as He loved us.

What of these saints who have been "born again" for years and years, but who still ignore Christ's strong teaching concerning the speck in another's eye, when there is a beam in our own?

What of the long-time believers who condemn certain behavior patterns in new Christians when their very condemnation is the direct opposite of what the Son of Man said He came to do? The Son of Man did not come to condemn the world, He came to save it, to identify with it. To heal it by reaching toward it with the offer of His own love and righteousness.

What of the corpulent saints who click their tongues disdainfully at social drinking, while licking their lips at the prospect of second helpings of the calorie-laden dessert?

What of the fevered, compulsive "soul-winning" efforts of the Christian businessman who underpays his employees and shades his income tax report?

What of the select little inner circles of evangelicals who not only refuse to extend normal human courtesy to other Christians who don't hold their exact marginal emphasis, but who blaze away at them in periodicals and from platforms? How do they resemble the Christ of the Cross who chose to come to the earth to die at a time when men were being crucified with their arms stretched out toward the whole world?

In short, what of those Christians who are tight-lipped, self-righteous, unloving, intolerant and critical? Are these persons born again? Yes, I believe they are. With all they knew of the nature of Christ, they have placed their faith in Him. And when anyone does this, He comes to live within.

However, *conversion* means that we turn around and go the other way. The human way is to condemn. The human way is to criticize and feel self-righteous. The human way is to become proud of religious self-effort and works, to be "justifiably" dishonest, to be gluttonous. And so, the kind conclusion, as I see it, is to realize that the saints who do not much resemble Jesus Christ in their life attitudes have not truly turned all the way around. They have not put their entire wills into their conversion.

Dr. Billy Graham once told me that he believes there are varying stages of conversion. This makes excellent sense to me. If conversion takes place in the conscious mind, then we are personally and individually responsible for the extent of it. Those uncontagious saints among us are merely those who, through self-love or off-center teaching, have not seen the necessity to turn around all the way, so that their inner attitudes are reversed also.

I do not doubt that they are born again. This is God's part. The new birth takes place in our unconscious and it is always the work of the Spirit. Conversion rests with us. God respects the choice of mankind. He could not change us in the depths, if He did not.

Christ may well have come to indwell the depths of a believer, but because He does respect our wills, we can refuse Him access to our conscious minds. They are under our control, if we are normal mentally. In a word, He can be "bottled up" in the depths by our un-Christlike conscious behavior patterns and attitudes.

The Christian who approaches life with a clenched fist is bottling up the Christ life within. This is his choice. He may go on doing it. But no one needs to go on showing no trace of a family resemblance to God, because when the new birth takes place, one is born of God into a new family. The Berkeley translation of John 1:12 and 13 is excellent. It declares what God has done for us, but it throws the weight of the *evidence* of His Presence directly upon us where it belongs: "To those who did accept Him, He granted *ability* to become God's children, that is, to those who believe in His name; who owe their birth neither to human blood, nor to physical urge, nor to human design, but to God."

We will go more deeply into this in Chapter 16. For now, "To those who did accept Him, He granted *ability* to become God's children." To bear a family resemblance to the Father. The extent of our resemblance to Him is directly involved in the extent of our conversion. We decide just how much we want to fall under His influence.

A child may be born of an earthly father and yet take none of his advice, cultivate none of his characteristics, refuse to obey him entirely in certain areas, and the old adage, "Like father, like son," falls apart!

In a letter I received only today as I write this chapter, a woman—newly wise in the true ways of the Lord Himself—although she has been a Christian for many years, wrote: "I came to my senses when, at last, my husband looked at me and shouted, 'I certainly don't want what you have!' He was the one I most longed to reach for Christ, but at that moment I saw that my religious ways were repellent to him. He didn't shout, 'I don't want *who* you have,' he said he didn't want *what* I had."

This woman's conversion, which began long ago, was extended in its scope when she saw this important truth. Conversion can and should be continuous. We do decide about our conversions. The first impetus toward Christian conversion springs from the Spirit. The initial call is from God. But a human being can be converted, as Dr. White pointed out, to any of a number of systems of thought aside from Christianity. The new birth, as spoken of by Jesus, is limited however, to contact with Christ as God in the flesh.

Perhaps those of you who read this book as new Christians also remember the time of your conversions. But there will be countless others who do not remember any conversion experience at all. I lovingly but definitely contend that if they believe in Christ, this does not mean they are not Christians and it does not indicate that they have not been born of God.

I am aware that some will disagree. This is all right. I am merely attempting to share what I have come to see as I have lived and studied and spoken with other Christians and with Christ during these last ten years. Here again is the dreadful danger of using our "boxes" to confine truths which cannot be confined. At least they cannot be confined without losing some of their value to us.

I am thinking now of several authentic Christians whom I know personally—some of them you would know —who cannot give an exact date of their conversion experience. Most of them were reared in authentically Christian homes. They have believed in Jesus Christ and followed Him from childhood. Their lives show that without a doubt they are converted, but they simply do not remember the time. Jesus made a clear point here, too: "By their fruits, ye shall know them."

Conversion comes slowly and gradually to some. This, too, depends largely upon the background, environmental influences and disposition of the person. But if their personalities show the fruits of a life lived with Christ, who can doubt the authenticity of their experiences?

To some, particularly those converted as adults, the road is so rough at times that the cry goes up, "I don't think I was ever really converted anyway!" By now, I've lost track of the number of times I've luxuriated in this misguided complaint. If we are genuinely concerned about our conversion, we can be pretty sure we are genuinely converted. Otherwise, we just wouldn't care. I must admit I have stopped indulging in this plaint since I have come to see the difference between the new birth and conversion. Because when I protested the authenticity of my conversion, although I didn't see it then, I was really only suspecting myself. I was responsible for the validity of my conversion. It took place in my conscious mind. But as long as I had the new birth confused with conversion, I felt relieved when I doubted my own experience, because although I might not have admitted it, I was really complaining that somehow God must not have done His part with me! Just because I was violently tempted to do something which I knew I should not do, I jumped quickly behind the cooked-up conclusion that probably "nothing" had really happened to me after all.

If only we could all see that it isn't a "thing" which happens to us anyway. It is a relationship into which we enter with a living Person. A Person who has said He will never leave us nor forsake us. So while the success or joy of my Christian life depends upon my cooperation with Christ, *my Christian life is Jesus Christ Himself.*

If He was telling the truth when He said, "Lo, I am with you always," then my tremblings and complaints about having lost "it" become the foolish mouthings of a person who is simply not thinking.

I may lose my joy, if I am ill or disobedient, or neglect my prayer-life and Bible study, but I cannot, no matter what I do, lose Christ—or He was misleading us when He said He would never leave us.

To another type of person, the mere mention of *conversion* is repulsive. He cringes in horror from the prospect of any deep emotional experience involving a religious belief. Actually, there are many professing Christians who take this view.

Dr. Ernest White says they pride themselves in "belonging to the class which William James in his book, *The Varieties of Religious Experience*, calls the healthy-minded, or the once born, in contradistinction to the sick-minded or the twice-born." [1]

Of these persons, Dr. White says, "Such people are unconsciously, or perhaps consciously, afraid of their own emotions, and have suppressed them to a large extent. They take an over-optimistic view of life and are either incapable of seeing the evil and shady side of life or they evade it by closing their eyes to it. They have never passed through the conflicts of mind which precede and lead up to conversion, and have therefore never felt the need for such an experience." [2]

The self-development cults by-pass the evils of sin and pain by simply denying that they exist at all. To all such people, Christian conversion seems both unreal and superfluous. They seem to be aware of no particular conflicts to be resolved, no disturbance of mind—with Pippa they smile and chant, "God's in His heaven, all's right with the world." As Dr. White describes them, "They are like a man who in the course of a journey comes to a hill which he must either climb or go around if he is to reach his journey's end. Instead of struggling on, he sits down at the bottom of the hill and whistles a merry tune, and persuades himself that the hill is not there at all." [3]

During the five years in which I directed the dramatic radio program *Unshackled,* I interviewed and wrote the script for the broadcast of over two hundred conversion stories. These were stories of men and women from all walks of life. In the main, they were persons who had turned to Christ at the Pacific Garden Mission in Chicago, after a varying number of years on Skid Row. I soon became aware, however, that we could easily be confusing certain of our listeners who had not shocked themselves or society by personalities gone out of control. Permission was given me then to dramatize stories, on occasion, which were more like those of our average listener.

Of course, I do not need to express my own conviction that conversion is needful. I am sure all of my other writings verify this. The changed direction of my own life verifies it. But from my observation during these past ten years, I am convinced that the actual types of conversion experiences vary almost as much as people vary.

The overly sensitive conscience may cause a violent emotional upheaval at conversion. The quiet, contained, balanced person in control of his personality patterns may come decisively, but silently and calmly, into the life with Christ. The important thing here is not that he is calm and quiet about it, but that the controlled personality needs a Saviour just as urgently as the cursing, uncontrolled, bottle-clutching man from Skid Row.

The emotional nature of a man's conversion to Christ seems to me to depend upon several things. If he has knowingly hurt and harmed many people, as had many of the persons whose stories I dramatized, I observed that there was great emotional conflict when he saw his sin, and great emotional relief when he recognized his forgiveness.

If the childhood of the convert was made fearful by a bad-tempered, violent father, the pre-conversion struggle to believe in God's love was often intense.

If the father happened to be a strict, domineering Christian legalist, who held a rod literally and figuratively over the son's head, then I discovered tears came quickly as the person whose story I was writing told me of his conversion. He would remember great trembling. "I shook like a leaf. I guess I was afraid of God. I thought He must be like Dad!"

Some told of great weeping before and after their conversions. These were usually men with heavy guilt on their consciences. Others wept before and laughed afterwards.

Another young man, not from the Mission, wrote the background of his own conversion story. It was beautifully done, with tasteful restraint. He was a Ph.D. and had come quietly and definitely into his commitment to Christ. The lack of emotional display in no way diminished his total surrender.

Some experienced conversion because of a quiet, deep, gnawing sense of need. Of something missing in their lives. Others experienced deep, shattering conviction of sin at the outset.

In my own conversion experience, I cannot honestly say I experienced remorse over sin in my life until a year later. Mine was a tricky mind. I had my conscience well under control. The trouble was, it was under my control. Therefore, it was out of tune with God's plan for me. Now, under His control, sin in my life causes me distress in a way I couldn't have coped with then. My own conversion was marked with a strange mixture of wonder at the possible discovery of God and a ghastly realization that I had lived my life cut loose from its moorings. My pre-conversion conflict was great. My conversion moment quiet and brief. And then great peace—and enthusiasm.

The actual mental conflicts and emotional reactions to conversion vary according to the temperament and background of the individual. What counts is the sincerity of our hearts—the total placing of our wills into His hands. This, too, comes slowly to some. And whatever the preconversion conflict, the important thing is that after conversion, after we have rested our case with Him, there is peace. There will be recurring conflict, but in the midst, peace with God.

We have Christ's own word for it that when we open the door, He will come in. The new birth is His work. And although we are empowered by the Holy Spirit to turn around and begin to follow Christ, the clean-cut results of our conversions are our conscious responsibility.

We are to stack our intellectual blocks in a corner and come as little children to the Father, in faith that we can know Him as He is in Jesus Christ. Forgiveness is the result of our asking. And the courage for our asking comes by faith in what we know His heart to be like.

We need to face the fact that although God always takes care of our new birth Himself, the success of our conversion depends upon our willingness to obey the One who has come to indwell us. We decide whether or not our conversion involves our total personalities.

Many people realize sin in their lives, come to the point of accepting Jesus Christ as their Saviour, and then turn back. Why is this?

I believe it is because, at that moment, the cost to them seems too high. It is true that Jesus told us that no wise man will build a house without counting the cost of it to himself. But it seems to me that those who turn back are, at least sometimes, victims of inadequate teaching about Jesus Christ. Somewhere along the line they have dragged along the too common concept that Christians are people who strive and strain "to do right." Nothing could be farther from the truth about the authentic Christian life. On the Cross God took full responsibility for every human being. "Surely He has borne our sicknesses and carried our sorrows . . . He was bruised for our iniquities; the punishment which procured our peace fell upon Him, and with His stripes we are healed. All we like sheep have gone astray; we have turned each one to his own way; and the Lord has laid on Him the iniquity of us all."

If we see clearly that the young Man on the Cross was God in the flesh, we see that God Himself laid on Himself our iniquity and our sorrows. He has taken full responsibility for us all. Those who turn back fail to realize that Jesus has invited us to get into the yoke with Him. Until we try out this invitation for ourselves, we somehow cannot quite believe that the burden does become light. Those who turn back have not seen Him as He is. They have not seen that He would ask nothing of us which He would not give us the power to do. They have not seen that He would ask nothing from us which would not be for our ultimate good. They have not realized that Good Friday is good because a completely good God hung on His Cross that day, revealing Himself clearly for the first time to everyone.

I almost turned back myself. Those moments of hesitation just before my final submission to Him stand out clearly to this day.

But I could not turn back. I was one of the fortunate ones who had been shown something of the true nature of God Himself, through Jesus Christ. At the moment of my turning I weighed the cost to me, but my thoughts were not whirling around a plan of salvation or a doctrinal emphasis or a fear of someone's concept of hell. They were whirling, I admit, but they were circling around Christ Himself. I merely had proven to me that afternoon in October, 1949, that Jesus knew what He said when He declared, "I, if I be lifted up . . . will draw all men unto me."

I had been pointed to Jesus Christ Himself, as God in the flesh. And I found Him irresistible.

# 16

# Have You Accepted Yourself
# As You Are?

# 16

---

## HAVE YOU ACCEPTED YOURSELF

## AS YOU ARE?

It is no secret that numbers of Christians do not live well-adjusted lives, in spite of their obviously sincere desire to do so. I am convinced that much of their trouble is based in the fact that they have not accepted themselves as they really are.

They spend hours in prayer and Bible reading, and travel hundreds of miles to listen to Christian speakers, but in their own strictly personal relationship with Christ they are dealing with one, and sometimes two, comparative unknowns: their own true nature and the true nature of Christ.

Much of the needless strain drops away when the believer begins to be realistic about the two involved in the Christian life. You are involved, and He is involved. When the two of you work realistically together, any problem can have a creative solution.

We have already established in Chapter 3 that He knows and accepts you as you are. But do you know yourself, and have you accepted yourself as you really are?

God will always do the best He can with us under all

circumstances. But as with the prodigal son (Chapter 5) we all need to "come to ourselves." We can remain unconsciously insincere and unrealistic even in our prayer lives unless we have an accurate estimate of our own personality twists and neuroses.

One sincere Christian woman I know prayed for years that her son-in-law would show her more love. That he would participate more freely in the family activities. Nothing whatever happened until this woman began to see that she, herself, was blocking the boy. She gave him money and a home, but unknowingly she "loved" the fellow from a pedestal. Her daughter, the boy's wife, had died in childbirth. The woman carried an unconscious resentment against him because she had advised them not to have another child. When the child was born, her daughter died. This resentment was easier for her to see, however, than the fact that her show of "love" toward her son-in-law had been all talk and gifts of money!

When she began to see herself realistically and to accept herself as a woman with a desperate need to stop trying to act as though she loved the boy, and to really include him in her life, she was free. She can laugh at herself now. And laughter at oneself is always proof that God has healed us in the touchy places.

Jesus said, "Blessed are the pure in heart, for they shall see God." At first glance, this seems almost a ridiculous thing to say. Is anyone ever pure in heart? If not, then does this mean that no one can ever really see God as He is?

No. It means that we can be *clear* in our motives. The simplest meaning of the word *pure* as it is used so often in the New Testament is *clear* or *clean*. Clean in the sense of being uncluttered.

I have been greatly helped by a book, *The Psychology of Jesus and Mental Health*, by Dr. Raymond L. Cramer. I wholeheartedly recommend it for anyone who is interested in genuine help toward Christian maturity. Pursuing this study of the meaning of the word "pure," Dr. Cramer writes: ". . . this word 'pure' as used in the Sixth Beatitude is derived from the same root as in 'catharsis'— meaning to cleanse or make pure. It refers to something that is free from that which would spoil or corrupt. The original Greek word meaning 'to cleanse' has reference in medical terminology to a purgative—a cathartic which cleanses or purges. The word 'catharsis' in psychological jargon describes a discharge of repressed ideas or emotions. Conflict is said to be eliminated by bringing the disturbed feature into consciousness and giving expression to it—spilling out the emotionally charged material." [1]

Dr. Cramer further explains that "there is no implication that merely telling someone else of our troubles or mistakes will have the desired effect because catharsis is possible only under permissive conditions."

He illustrates by saying that, in catharsis, the therapist's "calm, accepting manner is in direct contrast to the harsh condemnation that caused the individual to become so fearful that his unacceptable feelings were repressed beyond conscious awareness. No relief is secured by giving expression to the suppressed emotions if the listener shows signs of disapproval or shock."

It will do little or no good, then, if we spill out our problems to either overly sympathetic ears or to someone who is shockable. How simple it would seem to be if only the Christian would learn to spill out his troubles to God, who is always realistic, calm and accepting, and never shocked.

This does work when we do it honestly, calling our resentments by name, seeing ourselves as we are, admitting to our unloving natures, crying out to God to replace them with His own. But it is impossible for us to tell our real troubles even to God, when we don't know what they are ourselves. Or, worse still, when we catch a frightening momentary glimpse of ourselves and then rationalize it away!

If you are having trouble with another human being, the fault may lie mainly in the other person, but some of it is in you. I have never yet been involved with anyone in a difficult relationship in which the other person has been totally at fault. Perhaps my attitude is all that is wrong. I may be doing a seemingly magnificent job of being a spiritual "giant" by saying the right sounding things. But our attitudes always speak louder than our words. Especially if they are speaking to a disturbed personality.

"Blessed are the pure in heart, for they shall see God."

Dr. Cramer provocatively paraphrases the word "blessed" as used in the Beatitudes as "congratulations." So, congratulations to you if you have unmixed motives, because then you will be able to see through your own tangled attitudes—to God Himself. You will be clear in your heart, so you will be able to see God's way clearly and act clearly upon it.

If you are an hysterical, panicky, immature type of person, God's word cannot get through to you. You have listened too long to the sound of your own voice. It may be difficult for you to admit your immaturity and go to Him with it, talking with Him about it, but you must be willing to do this before He can answer your prayers to be rid of your present problems.

If the least little upsetting thing throws you into a rage, or causes you to lash out against someone else for causing your discomfort, you need to see in yourself the reason for such behavior. Your universe revolves around you, when it should revolve around God. You may not be able to help yourself, but God can help you—if you recognize and accept yourself as you are and begin to be honest with Him.

If you fill in every gap in an argument by running

yourself down, take stock! You are not only belittling God
by implying that He is unable to cope with your magnificent inferiority, you are probably trying to force someone
else to pay attention to you. Your motives are mixed.
You are not seeing yourself clearly.

If the slightest criticism throws you into a tirade of
self-defense, you cannot see God for looking at yourself.

The "pure in heart," those who are clear deep within
themselves, are those who will make an effort, at least, to
see themselves in their darkest need and accept what
they see as being true. Then, being able to see God, they
will see that the only thing to do is to throw themselves,
as they are, at the feet of Christ, as He is!

As long as we keep up one defense, He cannot do His
best for us. As long as we keep one eye covered where
our own sins and mistakes are concerned, He is blocked,
even though He longs to reconstruct our shabby personalities. As long as we justify one streak of bitterness on
our part, blaming it on someone else's mistreatment of us,
God must wait until we become honest before Him.

I do believe that there are some personalities so
twisted, so maladjusted, that they will need professional
help in seeing themselves as they are. In the majority of
cases, however, some honest study of the teachings of
Jesus, a period of time in prayer and self-examination
through the words of Paul in the thirteenth chapter of
I Corinthians, will show us, if we are willing to see, what
we are really like. We may see some of the defects in
other people, too, during this time, but this is not our
responsibility. Before any relationship can smooth out,
someone involved in it must—see God! Which means that
someone involved in it must be willing to have his inner
motives purified. Made clear.

Otherwise both parties will go on demanding of the
other what neither will be willing to give.

At the time of my conversion to Jesus Christ, I came

face to face with a woman with my name who was obviously concerned, above everything else, with relieving her own emotional needs in the pursuit of pleasure and stimulating people and work.

She was not concerned about people who needed her, she was concerned only about people who pleased or amused or benefited her in some way. She was not concerned about the work that needed to be done in the world, she was concerned only with the work that aroused her interest or paid her well. She was no longer concerned with thinking clearly and acting constructively, she was concerned with finding new forms of pleasure—travel, records, book collections, pedigreed dogs—anything that relieved her own emotional tensions for the moment.

When I came face to face with myself as I was, I wanted to do away with me. But there was the great Kindness all around me, and instead of annihilating myself I accepted myself as I was, a human being desperately in need of a Saviour. Facing myself clearly, I was able to see enough of God in Christ to know that He could change me into the kind of person He intended me to be in the first place!

When we give honest expression of the need in our own lives to God, we begin to experience healing.

Evil, according to Jesus, has to come from within. In Matthew 15:18, 19 we find Him declaring: ". . . what comes out of the mouth comes from the heart; that pollutes a man. For out of the heart come evil designs, murders, adulteries, sexual vices, thefts, lyings and slanders. These pollute a person; but to eat with unwashed hands does not pollute a person."

It is the condition existing at the center of our beings with which God must work. But in order that He can work, we must remove ourselves from the squirrel cage of spiritual techniques and begin to be realistic about what is within us.

Once we see ourselves realistically and accept what we see, then we are well on our way to realizing that God has already accepted us. According to the Sixth Beatitude, it is impossible to see God as He is until we have seen ourselves as we are. His love glows most brightly in the shadows of our need. Once I saw the depths of my own need and unworthiness, I was forced to allow Christ to stride out from among the religious old wives' tales where He is pictured as vengeful and remote. I was forced by the need in my own heart to realize that He didn't have to be entreated and cajoled and shouted at as I had heard done in my childhood. I was forced by the need in my own heart to look for Him at the only place where He can really be discovered—as He is—on the Cross with His arms stretched out, entreating all of us to come.

Sin has been defined as *missing the mark*. When we miss our mark in life, when we are unable to cope with the stresses and strains of life, it is due to the natural condition of man's heart, orbiting all alone—in some area, at least—disconnected from God.

The balanced, well-adjusted individual will be able to "roll with the punches" life hands him. If he is knocked down, he will get up and go on, accepting himself as a mere human being who is not and will not be perfect in this life. He will allow himself some failures, some grief, some disappointments. He will not blaze away at the circumstances or persons which cause his troubles. If he is downcast, he will accept the fact that God created all humanity with emotions which change. He will not leap to the egotistical conclusion that he is a singular victim borne down upon by a cruel world. If he is criticized, he may experience pain, but he will face the fact that his critics are the unpaid guardians of his soul. Perhaps there are grounds for their criticism, perhaps not. But if we have accepted ourselves as we are—human beings with enormous limitations and enormous potentials, we will expect enough, but not too much.

Actually, expecting too much of life and other people is in reality not expecting enough from God!

If you honestly see yourself now as being unable to cope with life, if you cannot "roll with the punches" it hands you, if you tend to berate and belittle yourself, if your outlook is gloomy and hopeless, if you set unreasonable goals for yourself and feel "put upon" because you do not reach them, if in a difficult human relationship you criticize and attempt to bring the other person down to your level of failure, then you have not accepted yourself realistically. None of these excessive responses to life linger for long in the personality of a person who has seen himself as he is, and has accepted himself as just another sin-distorted member of the human race in need of His creator's full life within him.

Dr. Cramer insists, and I believe rightly, that "emotionally disturbed persons are hopeless just as long as they think they are, and as long as they make no effort to change."

Jesus said, "Blessed are the hungry and thirsty for righteousness, for they shall be satisfied." Righteousness is rightness within and without. Integrity. A state of being complete, unmixed in our inner motives. The Bible tells us that we "are complete in Him." But reaching this state of completeness involves active participation from us. We learn to see God as He is, by learning to see ourselves as we are—incomplete without Him.

The very inadequacy of human nature points to the adequacy of God, or we live in an atmosphere of futility and treachery on the part of heaven!

When we stop to face the fact of the importance of one human personality to Jesus Christ, we are forced to face the fact that He offers the glorious potential of redeeming that human personality, or He was not who He claimed to be.

If you, right now, are claiming that your problems are unsolvable in Christ, you are inferring that Christendom is populated with idolaters.

All broken or damaged human relationships are merely outward signs of a lack of peace with God somewhere. The cause of the break with God may be an unconscious act or attitude on the part of the persons involved. But if we will come to Him honestly, confronting ourselves with the possibility that we have somewhere failed to be realistic about ourselves in the situation, He will show us.

"Wisdom from above" is a necessity if we are to adjust to the traumatic changes which life brings. But we do not get "wisdom from above" if we are not able to cope with it. There is a personal participation required here.

The Apostle James wrote, "Who among you is wise and understanding? Let him show by his good behavior that his actions are carried on with unobtrusive wisdom. But if you cherish bitter jealousy and rivalry in your hearts, do not pride yourselves in it and play false to the truth." Our actions and reactions show at once if we are making use of the "wisdom from above" which God has promised to anyone who asks. God does promise wisdom if we ask for it. "If any one of you lacks wisdom, let him ask God, who gives to everyone without reserve. . . ." But before He can give anything to us, we need to understand why we need it.

One good way to find out if you have truly accepted yourself as you are, and are making use of "wisdom from above" in your human relationships, is to meditate on this revealing passage in James' letter: "The wisdom from above is first of all pure [its motives are unmixed], then peaceable [without hidden barbs], courteous [kind], congenial [not self-defensive], full of mercy and good fruits [outgoing and Christ-like], impartial [fair-minded] and unpretentious [humble]."

Understanding does not necessarily imply approval, or sympathy, or agreement. Understanding is among the most misused of words. If a disturbed person constantly cries, "No one understands me!" the chances are that most people do. What that person is really saying is that no one sympathizes enough, no one does enough to make his life easier. There are many instances where one person misunderstands another, of course. But if this feeling of being misunderstood is a pattern, if the troubled person seems unable to find anyone who understands, it is quite likely that the difficulty lies in him. Understanding does not necessarily imply approval. It simply gives us a starting place.

From his years of counseling, both as a pastor and as a practicing psychologist, Dr. Raymond Cramer concludes that "The psychology of Jesus emphasizes facing reality, seeing one's self as a prerequisite to peace. The peacemaker faces problems, he does not avoid them . . . As we make peace with God, a change comes into our own lives and this is in turn reflected in the lives of other people. (Once) I have arrived at the state of being at peace with myself, at the center of my being, I can take a more normal attitude toward myself. People need no longer tiptoe around my personality!"

If people are forced to "tiptoe around" your personality, for your own sake *discover where you have failed to understand yourself.* Discover where you have failed to accept yourself as you are. Where you have failed to allow your own inner cleansing.

Once we have arrived at the place of being able to accept ourselves as we are, we automatically see our need for a deeper peace with God. A deeper commitment to Him and His methods of peaceful living. No one really sees himself as he is without seeing his own desperate need. At the point of need, the whole human race shares a common denominator.

And once we have seen and accepted ourselves as we are, we find it rather simple to see and accept other persons as they are. We stop feeling "put upon." We see that we mistreat and that we are mistreated by those who are as needy as we are. We see that we do not love adequately and are not loved enough. We see that we reject and that we are rejected. We see that we fail and so does everyone else.

God created a human family. And when it jerked itself loose from oneness with Him, it immediately took on one flagrant family trait—*need*. But there is no reason for desperation here. There is reason for rejoicing! Because all that anyone needs, to be filled with the fullness of God, is to recognize and accept his own need in the Presence of the One who can fill it.

In accepting our need, we accept ourselves. It is the essential self of the human being that needs the essential Self of God. And He has made Himself available to everyone.

# 17

## Have You Accepted Christ As He Is?

# 17

---

## HAVE YOU ACCEPTED CHRIST
## AS HE IS?

In this last chapter, as indeed throughout this book, I am not attempting to pose theological clarifications. Rather to clarify *life itself*, lived in an actual day-by-day personal relationship with God through Jesus Christ.

Literally millions of persons have "accepted Jesus Christ" as their Saviour, and in my mind there is no question but that He has done His part in the strictly personal transaction between Himself and each individual. Wherever a human heart is open to the invasion of Christ, He comes. The new birth takes place. But I can't help wondering how many persons have, from their side, consciously accepted Christ *as He really is*.

As I speak with Christians from all walks of life, I am constantly haunted by the idea that many of them have entered into some taught concept of what salvation is. This is good, but to me it lacks the dynamic of the expectant heart which opens itself to an eternal friendship with a God who has seen to it that He is discoverable to everyone.

Perhaps I can illustrate this way: When a man and

woman are married, it is not the marriage that gives them fulfillment, it is the joy of belonging to each other. It is the exchanged life. It is the tremendous potential that lies ahead in being able, at last, to live together. To share conflicts, agreements, little personal secrets, meals, bills, leaking roofs, new cars, failures, successes, tears, laughter, sandy beaches in summer and dreams before a fire in winter. *The dynamic lies in being able to share each other personally.*

In one sense, the marriage itself is an *explanation* of why they are at last able to belong to each other. To me, doctrines of the atonement and redemption, while necessary, are *explanations* of why we are at last able to be with God in the close, strictly personal relationship He intended when He created us.

Salvation is necessary, but the Saviour Himself is the dynamic. This may shock some persons, but I have seldom thought about my own salvation. I have been far too occupied with the Saviour Himself.

I realize that many who read this book will be those who have recognized their own disturbed symptoms in the preceding chapter. Some may be angry and rebellious and accuse me of describing their agony from a cold heart when I suggested repentance for their off-center attitudes. Some may be too disturbed to be able to take in what I said without extreme emotional involvement, which always blinds us to ourselves. Panicky, hysterical, depressed persons *are* sick emotionally. I have experienced genuine depressed moods myself and I have seen them in others. I did not write from a cold heart, but from a heart utterly convinced that if a troubled human being, alone or with the help of an understanding counselor, will expose his own heart as it is to the heart of Christ as it is, healing will begin.

In no way do I minimize the genuine suffering of those who feel unloved and who give vent to their agony by demanding attention and pleading for love from another human being. The need to be loved is without doubt the strongest drive in the human personality. When through circumstances we are deprived of the love we need, we are driven in one way or another to demand it.

But love that demands love in return never receives.

And here is the necessity for learning of Christ as He really is! Accepting Him realistically is the key that unlocks the door to the dynamic of a balanced, basically undisturbed personality for everyone.

As we learn the nature of God, we learn the nature of love. As we expose ourselves to His love, we find we are untangling at the center of our trouble areas. When we let Him love us all He wants to, we find ourselves learning how to show others the love that does not demand in return. Love that does not defend itself. Love that carries no grudges. Love that never tires of giving itself.

There is "no variableness, no shadow of turning" in God's love. Nothing that anyone can do or say or think can in any way alter the intensity and constancy of His love! His heart is every minute, under all circumstances, turned toward us. All of us.

I am convinced that He longs over and loves the most hardened heart in Communist Russia or China. I am convinced that He loves and yearns over the most ruthless convict in the death row of any prison. And I am convinced that He loves them each one as much as He loves me.

We as human beings cannot imitate the love of God in our daily lives. It is not a difference in degree between human love and God's love. It is a difference in kind. Human love, at its very best, thrives on response from the loved one. God's love would seem to thrive on suffering! From the Cross Jesus poured His love down upon His murderers because they needed it so much.

Human love, at its very best, is too often dependent

upon moods. God's love "is from everlasting to everlasting." Human love, at its very best, is in some measure exclusive. We find it easier to love those who agree with us, or who come from our background. God's love is all-inclusive. It is as wide as the stretched-out arms of the Cross of Christ.

As the mother finds it in her heart to give special attention to her crippled or retarded child, so God gives special attention to those whose needs are greater than the average.

Jesus said, "Blessed are they who mourn, for they shall be comforted." Dr. Cramer would paraphrase it, "Congratulations" if you have a serious problem, a gigantic heartache, a disturbed personality! God guarantees you His personal attention. Congratulations to all those who are in dire need! God has singled you out for comfort. And comfort does not mean He will give you a Bible verse that will temporarily calm you down. True comfort means that you can be changed, readjusted, matured, so that you will be able to meet life more comfortably.

Unless we know this about God's character, it is no wonder that we go on as though our "salvation" had to do only with some dim, distant entrance into heaven. It does have to do with our life forever in His presence, but it also has to do with our daily problems and personality twists right now.

If you are suffering under a constant irritation from the rough edges of your personality in an abrasive relationship with the rough edges of someone else's personality—perhaps under the same roof with you—congratulations! You automatically have God's full attention.

The Atonement of Jesus Christ was for all the world, but it was also specifically for you right now, in your circumstances. He laid His heart bare on the Cross so that you could find out His true intentions toward you. If you have accepted Him as He is—eagerly awaiting your willingness to let Him take you over in your trouble, you will begin to experience the comfort He promised. In fact, I don't think the Beatitudes are promises. I believe them to be statements of fact about the potential of the human life in harmony with the life of God under difficult circumstances.

If you have accepted Jesus Christ as He is, the pain you experience now, for example, because of the ungrateful behavior of your child, will not be less, but in it you will see the willingness of God to show you your child's personality disturbance as He sees it. You will see the willingness of God to show you your own personality disturbance which prevents peace, as He sees it.

If you have accepted Jesus Christ as He is, you will know already that He is, at all times, realistic. Entrance into the Kingdom of God, if we go in with our eyes open to the true nature of the King, is entrance into reality.

Over and over I speak with persons who have "accepted Christ as their Saviour" sincerely, and yet lug along with them heavy loads of guilt for old sins and mistakes. I do not question the salvation of these persons. But I do believe they have not accepted Him as He is. They have not really seen God as Jesus showed Him to be on the Cross. If we have accepted Christ as He is, we have also accepted His forgiveness.

One deep look into the heart that was torn open on Calvary shows us irrevocably that He is a forgiving God. Turn the word "forgive" around, and it reminds us that here is Someone who loved us enough to *give for* us His very life! Forgiveness is a part of the very nature of God Himself. Just as love is. There is no love apart from forgiveness. *If we still feel guilt, we are declaring God to be unloving.*

To carry guilt brings great pain and suffering. And when we are in pain, we resent having our pain treated realistically. We prefer sympathy and mere words of comfort. God does not mistreat us with this kind of easy pampering. He wants us to be healed. And so, to you who still carry guilt feelings even after you have linked your life with the life of Christ, He says, "If you cling to this guilt after what I have done for you, you doubt My love. I have gone all the way to show you what I am really like. Please look, my child. Please look!"

Obviously God came in the Person of Jesus Christ so that we could be reunited with Him for all eternity. But this reuniting begins now. Jesus didn't go about urging people to come to Him in order that they could be given an eternal insurance policy. This is part of it, but His emphasis is always on Himself. On His Person. He didn't declare, "I, if I be lifted up from the earth, will draw all men unto me," so that orthodox Christianity would have a proof text! He said it because He knew that once men and women *saw Him as He is,* they would be unable to turn away from Him.

I do not believe that I will spend eternity in His Presence because that is one of the tenets of the orthodox Christian faith. I believe it because of what I have learned about the character of the One who said it.

I do not believe that if I will be honest with Him in the realization of my needs, He will be able to cope with the twists in my personality merely because I have read the Beatitudes. I believe it because of what I have learned about the nature and intentions of the One who voiced them.

I do not believe I am forgiven because of a theological statement about the atoning work of Jesus Christ. I believe I am forgiven because of what I have learned of the heart of the One who made the atonement possible.

My spiritual certainties are not due to some special religious agility on my part. They are due to my *continuing discovery of what God is really like in Jesus Christ.*

My prayer life is effective, but not because I am, by

nature, diligent. In fact, I find it just as difficult as you do to take time from a busy schedule. But my prayer life deepens and I begin to understand the meaning of unceasing prayer, as I continue my discovery of the nature of the One to whom I pray.

In her excellent book, *Prayer—Conversing with God*, Rosalind Rinker writes, "Prayer is a dialogue between two persons who love each other." [1]

As I realize His love for me, I find myself returning my love to Him with no conscious effort on my part. He draws love from me because of what He is like. And when I love, I find myself longing to converse with my loved one. I pray because of what I know Jesus Christ to be like. I have found Someone who not only hears and understands, but who can do something about my situation, and my human nature.

Constantly, Christians are urged to witness for Jesus Christ. I have never understood the necessity for this urging. I fully understand the necessity for witnessing, but if we have accepted Him as He is, if we really see His nature, His intentions toward us, His heart—how can we not talk about Him? I find that He walks quite naturally into almost any conversation. No virtue or special zeal is required of me. I am merely convinced of who He is and of what He is like.

I have no idea how many persons have met Christ through some word of mine. I do not keep myself whipped up into a bundle of taut nerves in an effort to win people to Jesus Christ. I have begun, at least, to see something of His intense desire to have them as His own. He makes the openings and, when He makes them, they are openings into hearts. Not mere opportunities for me to talk.

Those who have accepted Jesus Christ as He is are natural people at last. It has been said that once we have been invaded by the supernatural, through the Spirit of

Christ, we are, at last, truly natural. I believe this. I have experienced it. Those who have accepted Christ as He is are not tense and tired, nor tiring. The Christ-adjusted personality is calm and sure and contagious.

He did not say, "Come unto me all ye that labor and are heavy laden and I will give you sleepless nights and anxiety over winning souls." He said, "Come unto me . . . and I will give you rest." He did not say, "My yoke will drag you along at a break-neck speed and my burden will lay on you the responsibility for winning everyone you meet." He said, "My yoke is easy and my burden is light."

I have discovered, in my own life at least, that many more people are attracted to Christ since I have taken His advice and learned more of Him as He is. Human hearts resist pressure from another human being. But the Spirit of Christ moves quietly and deeply, with the sure motion of eternity. Only He knows how to open hearts to Himself.

I am aware that there will be many who read this book who have not accepted Jesus Christ at all.

Perhaps you are one of these. Perhaps, by now, you too have found reality in His words, "I, if I be lifted up . . . will draw all men unto me."

Perhaps you now want to belong to Him.

If you do, you can be sure that your desire to enter into this glorious relationship is His doing! Even the restless longing in your heart is inspired by Christ. You want Him because He has at last gotten through to you with the intense longing in His own heart over you, personally.

If you are aware of His love for you, if your heart has been stirred to respond to this love, *your first conscious response is all that remains to be done.* Right now, as you are, wherever you are, you can begin to respond to Jesus Christ. You may want to put it into words. You may want to cry out to Him, "Lord, I believe; help thou my unbelief!" You may want to tell Him in words that you have seen the futility of living your life cut off from His life. You may want to express in words to Him your "godly sorrow" for your sins. This is a relieving thing to do. But if you are experiencing repentance in your heart as you are there with Him now, He knows it.

Perhaps you have never prayed before. Prayer is no particular art. It is merely talking to the One who has loved you from the beginning. You can feel at home with Him. Express yourself any way that seems natural to you. It is the intention of your heart that matters, and He knows your heart exactly as it is. He knows the depths of your need. The depths of your sin. And He knows the depths of your sincerity toward Him.

If you feel a desire to turn to this Christ of the Cross now, you can be sure that in you is already the power to do it. He has seen to this. If you feel an inward struggle, it will not mean that He is resisting you. He is love, and as love, He is always in motion toward you. Becoming a Christian has been described as, "shifting the central confidence of our lives from ourselves to the Person of Jesus Christ." This you alone can do. You can begin now, to rest your case—all of it, with Him.

If only the word "yes" escapes your lips, that is enough. If only your heart begins to agree with Him, that is enough.

And when you accept Him, *accept Him as He is*, knowing that He has accepted you, exactly as you are. The moment you begin, by faith, to walk with Him, you can be absolutely sure that He has begun with you. "Behold, I stand at the door and knock. If any man will open the door, *I will come in.*"

Any human heart who sees Christ at last as God Himself, with His arm stretched out on the Cross for love of us, has only to say, "Lord, thank You for having become forever personally involved with me. From now on, by

Your grace, I mean to be forever personally involved with You."

At this moment of turning, there begins eternal life.

There begins the integration of a once divided heart.

There begins the promised new life.

There begins the end of the lonely way.

There begins the strictly personal relationship with the One who Himself is the beginning and the end.

There begins the great adventure of discovering God as He really is in Jesus Christ.

There begins the transforming friendship with God Himself.

And, at this expectant moment, the invaded heart now hears and recognizes the Voice of the One who says, "I no longer call you servants, for a servant does not know what his master is working out; but I have called you friends . . . You have not chosen Me, but I have chosen you and I have appointed you to go out and produce fruit and keep on producing, so that whatever you may ask the Father in My name He may grant you."

"I will certainly not cast out anyone who comes to Me."

# REFERENCE NOTES

CHAPTER 9

1. J. B. Phillips, *Your God Is Too Small* (New York: Macmillan Co.) pp. 37-38. Used by permission.

CHAPTER 12

1. A. Maeder, *Ways to Psychic Health* (New York: Charles Scribner's Sons, 1953) pp. 177-178. Used by permission.
2. Ibid., p. 194.

CHAPTER 14

1. Ernest White, *Christian Life and the Unconscious* (New York: Harper & Brothers, 1955) pp. 29-30. Used by permission.
2. Ibid., p. 33.

CHAPTER 15

1. Ernest White, *Christian Life and the Unconscious* (New York: Harper & Brothers, 1955) p. 45. Used by permission.
2. Ibid., p. 45.
3. Ibid., p. 46.

CHAPTER 16

1. Raymond L. Cramer, *The Psychology of Jesus and Mental Health* (Los Angeles: Cowman Publications, 1960) pp. 117, 175-176, 220-221, 223. Used by permission.

CHAPTER 17

1. Rosalind Rinker, *Prayer—Conversing with God* (Grand Rapids: Zondervan Publishing House, 1959) p. 23.

# RECOMMENDED READING

## GENERAL

Cramer, Raymond, *The Psychology of Jesus and Mental Health* (Los Angeles: Cowman Publications), 1960.

Lewis, C. S., *Mere Christianity* (New York: Macmillan Co.).

Phillips, J. B., *When God Was Man* (New York–Nashville: Abingdon Press).

Phillips, J. B., *Your God Is Too Small* (New York: Macmillan Co.).

Phillips, J. B., *Is God At Home?* (New York–Nashville: Abingdon Press).

Phillips, J. B., *The New Testament in Modern English* (New York: Macmillan Co.).

Siewert, Frances E., Ed., *The Amplified New Testament* (Grand Rapids: Zondervan), 1958.

Simpson, P. Carnegie, *The Fact of Christ* (London: James Clarke and Co., Ltd.).

Verkuyl, Gerrit, Ed., The Berkeley Version of the Holy Bible (Grand Rapids: Zondervan), 1959.

White, Ernest, *Christian Life and the Unconscious* (New York: Harper & Brothers), 1955.

## DEVOTIONAL

Chambers, Oswald, *My Utmost for His Highest* (New York: Dodd Mead).

Kelley, Thomas, *A Testament of Devotion* (New York: Harper & Brothers).

Price, Eugenia, *Share My Pleasant Stones* (Grand Rapids: Zondervan), 1957.

Rinker, Rosalind, *Prayer—Conversing with God* (Grand Rapids: Zondervan), 1959.

Smith, Hannah Whitall, *The Christian's Secret of a Happy Life* (Westwood, N. J.: Fleming H. Revell).

180

CPSIA information can be obtained
at www.ICGtesting.com
Printed in the USA
JSHW030513250221
12032JS00001BA/36